AFRICAN SAFARI:

THE COMPLETE TRAVEL GUIDE TO TEN TOP GAME VIEWING COUNTRIES

BY
MARK NOLTING

Library of Congress Cataloging-in-Publication Data

Nolting, Mark, 1951 -
    African safari.

    Includes index.
    1. Wildlife watching -- Africa, Sub-Saharan -- Guide-
books. 2. Safaris -- Africa, Sub-Saharan -- Guide-books.
3. National parks and reserves -- Africa, Sub-Saharan --
Guide-books. 4. Africa, Sub-Saharan -- Description and
travel -- 1981 -   -- Guide-books.   I. Title.
QL337.S78N65 1987 916.7'04   87-8481
ISBN: 0-939895-00-5 (alk. paper)

ISBN: 0-939895-00-5

Maps and Drawings by Deborah C. DeSantis

Cover Art by Danny Atchley

Produced by Wright & Ratzlaff Associates

Printed in the United States of America

Second Printing

TO MY PARENTS
FOR ENCOURAGING ME TO TRAVEL
AND FOR THE REWARDING LIFE I HAVE LED
AS A RESULT OF THAT ENCOURAGEMENT

ACKNOWLDEGMENTS

The completion of this guide would not have been possible without the assistance and expert advice of the many people. Many thanks to all who have contributed to this project, including the following:

Ms. Chawa Bagosi and the Botswana Division of Tourism, Sue Carver of Bonaventure Travel, and Penny and Paul Rawson; Burundi National Office of Tourism; Sam Okungu and Maggie Maranga of the Kenyan Tourist Office, Kenya Ministry of Tourism and Wildlife, Alnoor Dossa of Ivory Safaris, Dick and Adam Hedges of Safari Camp Services, Alan Dixon of Let's Go Travel, Nani Croze, Alex and Sally Braguine of Adventure Associates and Tom Matsalia of Kenya Railways; Lesotho Tourist Board and Niel van Schalkwyk of Overland Safaris; Roselyne Hauchler and the Mauritius Government Tourist Office, White Sands Tours; Peter McDonald, Wikkie Van Rooyen and Peter Voight of the Namibia Directorate of Trade and Tourism and Henry Dames of the SWA Publicity and Tourist Association; Rwanda Office of Tourism and Maurice Bare of Rwanda Travel Service; H. G. Dettweiler and Sakkie Hatting of the South African Tourist Board, Margaret Kinsman of Comair, Hennie Stoman of South African Airways, Alan Simpson of The Travel Shop, Afro Ventures, Jenni Nathanton of Bushvelt Safaris, Louise Nicholson of SarTravel, Fred Marillier of S.A. Railways, Melanie Millen, Barbara Ickinger and Tony Lanza of Sun International, Gail Wight-Staver, Mike Donaghy and Paul CH Van Wijk; Swaziland Government Tourist Office and Reuben Mapalala; Ellison Malekia of the Tanzania Office of Tourism, Mr. Macha and Mr. Mpumilwa of the TTC, David Bygott, N.V. Patel of Kearsley Tours and Mr. Fikirini of the Tanzania Friendship Tourist Bureau; Uganda Ministry of Tourism and Wildlife and Ugandan Hotels Corporation; Victor and Brigitte Ngezayo, and

Marcel Dony of Amiza Travel; Margaret Makungo and the Zambia National Tourist Board, Mr. Vibetti and Tony O'Brian of Zambia Airways, W.P. Sodala and Eagle Travel, Susan Victor of Andrews Travel, Angus and Rosemary Bradshaw, Charley Ross and John Yost of Sobek; Zimbabwe Tourist Development Corporation, Leslie Kripps of Safari Interlink (Travel Agency), Ian Cochrane of UTC, Ted Nelson of Air Zimbabwe, Jeanette Creewel of Zimbabwe Sun Hotels and U.S. Ambassador David Miller; Nigel Page and Tertius van Zyl and British Airways.

Special thanks to Sue and Steve Soldoff of Sue's Safaris and Jim Heck of Explorer's World Travel for their expert advice and comments in reviewing this guide, to Maryann Watson for accompanying me on part of my journey and providing hundreds of excellent photographs used in our seminars.

In addition, Bryan and Jo Hanson, NoorJehan Dhanani, John Hatt, Hilary Bradt, Jürg and Barbara Lichtenegger and my other dear European friends and world travelers for their advice and assistance.

Very special thanks go to Mike and Kathy Eldon and family, and Andre and Gendika Louw and family who most generously provided me with a "home away from home," as well as valuable advice and friendship which will always be remembered and appreciated.

My eternal thanks to Deborah DeSantis for her beautifully sensitive illustrations, helpful suggestions and encouragement throughout the course of the project.

CONTENTS

TO THE READER

NOTE: Population pressures in Africa are causing many parks to be reduced in size, resulting in even further declines in wildlife. African governments must be able to prove to their people that the parks provide more jobs, foreign exchange and other benefits than if the land were given to them for farming or grazing. By traveling to these countries and visiting the parks and reserves, you will be making a significant contribution to the conservation of endangered wildlife by helping prove the economic viability of protecting some of the world's most unique wildlife. This may be the most personally rewarding gift you have ever made!

A REQUEST: Please write and tell us about your trip, including the highlights of your vacation, opinions of accommodation, transportation, tour operator, etc., so we may best help future travelers through accurate updates of this guide and through Global Travel Consultants' African Travel Service (P. O. Box 2587, Pompano Beach, FL 33072; tel: 305-781-3933).

For your convenience, an information form has been provided for you on the third to the last page of this book. Photocopy the form, fill it out and mail it to us as soon as possible after your trip to Africa is completed.

CALL OF THE WILD

CALL OF THE WILD

Feature films like the "African Queen" and "Out of Africa" have kindled in the hearts of many people a flame of desire for travel to Africa.

A visit to Africa allows you to experience nature at its finest — almost devoid of human interference, living according to a natural rhythm of life that has remained basically unchanged since the beginning of time.

At our deepest roots, the African continent communicates with our souls. Travelers return home, not only with exciting stories and adventures to share with friends and family, but with a feeling of accomplishment, increased self-confidence and broader horizons from having ventured where few have gone. Here's the kind of adventure about which many dream but which few experience.

Having visited Africa once, you too will want to return again to the peace, tranquility and adventure it has to offer. I invite you to explore with me the reasons for this never ceasing pull as we journey to some of the most fascinating places on earth.

The time to visit Africa is now. In spite of international efforts, poaching is still rampant. In addition, the continent is rapidly becoming westernized, making it more and more difficult to see the indigenous peoples living as they have for thousands of years. Go now, while Africa can still deliver all that it promises — and more!

MAP OF AFRICA

(EAST, CENTRAL & SOUTHERN)

African Safari highlights and compares wildlife reserves and other major attractions in ten of the continent's top game viewing countries along with four other countries of great interest to travelers.

Most people travel to Africa to see lion, elephant, rhino, and other wildlife unique to this fascinating continent in their natural surroundings. **African Safari** makes planning your adventure of a lifetime easy.

Africa is huge. It is the second largest continent, covering over 20% of the world's land surface. More than three times the size of the United States, it is also larger than Europe, the United States and China combined. No wonder it has so much to offer!

After an exhilarating day on a photographic safari many guests return to revel in the day's adventures over exquisite European cuisine in deluxe camps and lodges. In addition, this captivating guide presents many options for the special interest traveler.

From the easy-to-read "When's the Best Time to Go" chart you can conveniently choose the specific reserves and country(ies) that are best to visit during your vacation period.

The glossary contains words commonly used on safari as well as words and phrases in French and Swahili. English is the major language in most of the countries covered in this guide, so language is in fact not a problem. The "Safari Pages" (safari directory) provide a veritable gold mine of difficult-to-find information and sources on Africa.

This guide is designed to help you decide where is the best place to go in Africa to do what you want to do, when you want to do it, in a manner of travel that personally suits you best.

African Safari is actually a travel kit, providing you with convenient access with everything you need in order to enjoy the vacation of a lifetime.

First, read this book. Then contact a travel agent who knows Africa or get in touch with the experts at Global Travel Consultants, Pompano Beach, Florida, for their wide-ranging advice on African travel.

WHEN'S THE BEST TIME TO GO?

The "When's the Best Time to Go?" chart shows at a glance when to go to best enjoy the countries, parks and reserves of your choice, and the best places to go in the month(s) in which your vacation is planned. In other words, how to be in the right place at the right time.

For example, your vacation is in February and your primary interest is game viewing on a photographic safari. Find the countries on the chart in which game viewing is "excellent" or "good/fair" in February. Turn to the respective country chapters for additional information and choose the ones that intrigue you the most. Use this chart as a general guideline; conditions vary from year to year.

In this guide, **game viewing** and **wildlife viewing** are used interchangeably. **Game** traditionally refers to animals that are hunted for sport but is also the term generally used in the travel industry when referring to photographic safaris to wildlife areas. This guide is about observing and photograph-ing wildlife — not hunting.

Timing can make a world of difference. For example, Hwange National Park in Zimbabwe is well known for its 9,000+ elephant population. I recently spent Christmas there (during

WILDLIFE AREAS

WHEN'S THE BEST TIME TO GO?

Use the chart below as a general guideline as to the best time for game viewing, keeping in mind that conditions vary from year to year.

Excellent △   Good/Fair •   Poor X

COUNTRY	WILDLIFE AREAS	JAN	FEB	MAR	APR	MAY	JUN	JUL	AUG	SEP	OCT	NOV	DEC
Botswana	Chobe, Moremi & Okavango Delta	X	X	X	X	•	•	△	△	△	•	X	X
	Nxai Pan & Makgadikgadi	•	△	△	•	X	X	X	X	X	X	•	•
Kenya	Amboseli	△	△	△	•	•	•	△	△	△	△	•	•
	Masai Mara	△	△	△	•	•	•	△	△	△	△	•	•
	Meru & Samburu	△	△	△	•	X	•	△	△	△	△	•	•
	Tsavo (West & East)	△	△	△	•	X	•	△	△	△	△	•	•
Namibia	Etosha & Namib-Naukluft	X	X	X	X	•	•	△	△	△	△	•	X
Rwanda	Akagera	•	•	•	X	•	•	△	△	△	•	•	•
	Volcano	△	•	•	△	△	△	△	△	△	•	•	•
So. Africa	Kruger & Private Res.	X	X	X	X	•	△	△	△	△	•	X	X
Tanzania	Lake Manyara & Ngorongoro Crater	△	△	△	•	•	△	△	△	△	△	△	•
	Serengeti	△	△	△	△	△	△	•	•	•	•	△	△
	Ruaha & Selous	•	•	•	X	X	•	△	△	△	•	X	•
	Tarangire	•	•	•	•	X	△	△	△	△	△	•	•
Uganda	Murchison Falls	△	△	△	•	•	•	•	X	X	X	X	X
	Ruwenzori	△	△	△	•	•	△	△	△	△	X	•	△
Zaire	Kahuzi-Biega	X	X	X	•	△	△	△	△	•	•	X	X
	Virunga	△	△	•	X	X	△	△	•	•	•	△	△
Zambia	Kafue & S. Luangwa	X	X	X	X	X	•	△	△	△	•	X	X
Zimbabwe	Mana Pools, Hwange Matusadona	X	X	X	X	X	•	△	△	△	△	X	X

the rainy season) and we didn't see one elephant. But during the dry season, they're everywhere.

In most cases the best game viewing, as exhibited on the chart, also corresponds to the dry season. Wildlife concentrates around waterholes and rivers and vegetation is less dense than in the wet season, making game easier to find. There are, however, exceptions. For instance, the Serengeti migration often begins at the height of the rains in Tanzania.

During the rainy season the land is often luxuriously green, the air clear. People with dust allergies may wish to plan their visits soon after the rains have started. Game is more difficult to find but there may be fewer travelers in the parks and reserves.

The best times for birdwatching are often the opposite of the best times for big game viewing. Birdwatching, however, is fairly good year-round in many regions.

THE SAFARI EXPERIENCE

"Alephaant, allephanntt", the Masai softly said as he escorted us to dinner that evening. Neither of us could understand him until he shined his flashlight on a tree-sized elephant browsing not 50 feet from where we stood. It was then I realized why we were requested to wait for the spear-wielding Masai assigned to our tent to escort us to dinner. The pathway to the dining tent was covered with giant pizza-sized footprints that had not been there 45 minutes earlier. Carrying a spear in these parts is not a bad idea!

The dining tent was filled with people from the four corners of the earth, reveling in camaraderie and sumptuous cuisine by candlelight. An excellent selection of wines and desserts complemented the meal.

After dinner we sat around a roaring fire, drinking whiskey, listening to bush lore from our entertaining host. We retired to our very comfortable deluxe tent with private facilities, and later watched hippo grazing only a few feet from our tent. The night was alive with the sounds and scents of the Africa we had dreamed of — the untamed wilderness where man is but a temporary guest and not a controller of nature.

At 05:30 the next morning I was awakened by steaming hot coffee brought to my bedside by my private tentkeeper. Soon we were off at 06:00 for a short game drive to where the hot-air balloons were being filled. Moments later we lifted above the plains of the Masai Mara for the ride of a lifetime.

Silently viewing game from the perfect vantage point, we brushed the tops of giant acacias for close-up views of birds' nests and baboons. Most animals took little notice, but somehow the hippos knew we were there. Maybe it was our shadow, or the occasional firing of the burners necessary to keep us aloft.

Our return to earth was an event in itself. One hour and 15 minutes after lift-off our pilot made a perfect crash landing. By the way, all landings are crash landings, so just follow your pilot's instructions and join in the fun.

Minutes later a champagne breakfast appeared on the open savannah within clear view of herds of wildebeest, buffalo and zebra. Our return to camp was another exciting game drive, only a little bumpier this time.

Most game drives last a few hours and are made in early morning, often before breakfast, in late afternoon and at night (where allowed) when the wildlife is most active.

For those who do not prefer tented camps there are hotels and lodges ranging from comfortable to deluxe in or near most parks and reserves. Many properties have air-conditioning, swimming pools and one or more good restaurants and bars. Going on safari can be a very comfortable, fun-filled adventure!

WILDLIFE

Animals are most often found in and nearby the habitats in which they feed or hunt. These habitats fall roughly into four categories — savannah, desert, wetlands and forest.

Savannah is a very broad term referring to dry land which can be open grasslands, grasslands dotted with trees, or wooded areas. Grazers (grass-eaters) and carnivores (meat-eaters) adept at hunting in savannah are most easily found here. Some browsers (leaf-eaters) also make the savannah their home.

Deserts have little or no standing water and very sparse vegetation. Many desert animals do not drink at all but derive water only from the plants they eat. Some savannah grazers

White Rhino

and carnivores can be found in the desert.

African **forests** are thickly vegetated, often with grasses and shrubs growing to about 10 feet in height, shorter trees 20-50 feet high, and a higher canopy reaching to 150 feet or more.

It is usually more difficult to spot animals in forests than in the other habitats. Many forest animals such as the elephant are more easily seen in open savannah areas adjacent to forests. Forest herbivores (plant-eaters) are browsers, preferring to feed on the leaves of plants and fruits usually found in forests. Carnivores have adapted to a style of hunting where they can closely approach their prey under cover.

Wetlands consist of lakes, rivers and swamps which often are part of a larger savannah or forest habitat. Many rivers wind through savannah regions, providing a habitat within a habitat. Wetlands are good places not only to see wetland species but also other habitat species that come there to drink.

The major parks and reserves listed on the following pages are classified according to their most dominant habitat. Use the "Wildlife Areas by Habitat" and "Animals by Habitat" charts as a rough guide in finding the parks and reserves that

ANIMALS BY HABITAT

The animals listed below are classified according to the habitat where most of their time is spent. The animals are listed in order of size by weight.

SAVANNAH

Grazers:
white rhino
eland
zebra
waterbuck
roan
sable
gemsbok (oryx)
topi
hartebeest
wildebeest
tsessebe
warthog
reedbuck
Grant's gazelle
impala
springbok
Thomson's gazelle

gerenuk
klipspringer
steenbok

Browsers:
giraffe
black rhino
kudu
dikdik

Carnivores:
lion
hyena
cheetah
African wild dog
jackal
mongoose
bat-eared fox

FOREST

Browsers:
elephant
nyala
bongo
bushbuck
duiker

Primates:
gorilla
baboon
chimpanzee

colobus monkey
sykes monkey

Carnivores:
leopard
serval
genet

ANIMALS BY HABITAT

WETLANDS

Grazers:
hippopotamus
buffalo
sitatunga

Carnivores:
crocodile
otter

DESERTS

see Savannah
grazers and
carnivores above

WILDLIFE AREAS BY HABITAT

Savannah Wildlife Areas

Botswana
Chobe

Kenya
Amboseli
Masai Mara
Meru
Nairobi
Samburu
Tsavo

Namibia
Etosha

Rwanda
Akagera

South Africa
Kruger
Private Res.

Tanzania
Mikumi
Ngorongoro
Ruaha
Selous
Serengeti
Tarangire

Zaire
Virunga (Rwindi)

Zambia
Kafue
South Luangwa

Zimbabwe
Hwange
Matopos

Forest Wildlife Areas

Kenya
Aberdare
Mt. Elgon
Mt. Kenya

Rwanda
Volcano

Tanzania
Arusha
Gombe Stream
Mt. Kilimanjaro

Zaire
Kahuzi-Biega
Virunga (other)

WILDLIFE AREAS BY HABITAT

Wetland Wildlife Areas

Botswana
Moremi
Okavango Delta

Kenya
Lake Baringo
Lake Borgoria
Lake Nakuru
Lake Naivasha

Tanzania
Lake Manyara

Uganda
Murchison Falls
Ruwenzori N.P.

Zambia
Kafue

Desert Wildlife Areas

Namibia
Namib-Naukluft
Skeleton Coast

Botswana
Kalahari Desert

are most likely to have the animals you are most interested in seeing on safari.

Many of these wildlife areas are composed of more than one habitat, so consult the text for in-depth descriptions. Keep in mind that savannah and forest animals visit wetland habitats to drink and that many forest animals are more easily seen on the open savannah.

A well-rounded safari includes visits to at least three types of habitats and parks, giving the visitor an overall picture of the wildlife and ecosystems.

RULES & REGULATIONS

Wildlife reserves differ greatly in their rules and regulations. Three regulations that may affect your choice of parks to visit are the type of vehicles allowed and whether or not night safaris or walking safaris are permitted.

Open **vehicles** usually have two or three rows of elevated seats behind the driver's seat. There are no side or rear windows or permanent roof, providing unobstructed views in all directions and a feeling of being part of the environment instead of on the outside looking in. This is my favorite type vehicle for viewing wildlife. When near lion the engine is kept running to allow quick get-aways in case the predators approach too closely.

In vehicles with roof hatches or pop-top roofs, riders stand up through the hatch for great photographic opportunities. If the vehicle is full, riders usually must take turns using the hatches, making tours which guarantee window seats for every passenger (i.e. maximum of seven passengers in a 9-seat mini-van) all the more attractive.

Wildlife viewing, and especially photography, are more difficult where closed vehicles are required.

Night game drives open a new world of adventure. Nocturnal animals, seldom if ever seen by day, are viewed with the aid of the vehicle's powerful search light. Bushbabies, night apes, leopard, and many other species can be seen.

In addition to the chart that follows, night game drives are allowed and often conducted outside of many reserves, including the Masai Mara (Kenya) and Hwange, Mana Pools and Matusadona (Zimbabwe).

Walking safaris put one in closest touch with nature.

VEHICLES - NIGHT GAME DRIVES - WALKING SAFARIS

COUNTRY	PARK OR RESERVE	TYPE VEHICLE ALLOWED			NIGHT DRIVES	WALKING SAFARIS
		OPEN	ROOF HATCHES	CLOSED		
Botwsana	Chobe	X				
	Moremi	X				X
	Okavango	X			X	X
Kenya	Tsavo		X			X
	Other Parks		X			
Namibia	Etosha			X		
Rwanda	Akagera		X			
	Volcano	X				X
S. Africa	Kalahari-Gemsbok			X		
	Kruger			X		X
	Private Reserves	X			X	X
Tanzania	Selous		X			X
	Other Parks		X			
Uganda	Q. Elizabeth Murchison Falls		X			
Zaire	Kahuzi-Biega	X				X
	Virunga		X			
Zambia	Kafue & S. Luangwa	X			X	X
Zimbabwe	Hwange		X			
	Mana Pools & Matusadona	X				X

Suddenly your five senses come alive — every sight, sound and smell becomes intensely meaningful. Could that be a lion in the dense brush ahead? I wonder how long ago these rhino tracks were made? Can that herd of elephant see or smell us approaching?

Accompanied by an armed wildlife expert, walking safaris last anywhere from a few hours to several days. The bush can be examined up close and at a slower pace, allowing more attention to its fascinating detail than on a safari by vehicle.

Participants can often approach quite closely to game, depending on the direction of the wind and the cover available. This is experiencing the excitement and adventure of the bush at its best. Zambia is the top destination for walking safaris. See the chapter on Zambia for details.

ACCOMMODATION

Most areas of greatest interest to tourists have comfortable hotels, lodges and/or tented camps specifically designed to cater to the discerning traveler's needs.

The word "camp" often refers to lodging in chalets, bungalows or tents in a remote location. Deluxe tented camps often have better service, food — and certainly a truer safari atmosphere than most hotels.

Hotels in the larger cities are categorized as **Deluxe, First Class** and **Tourist Class,** while lodges and tented camps are classified as **Class A — F**. Keep in mind that many lodges and tended camps are located in wildlife areas 3,000 feet or more above sea level, so air conditioning (a/c) is often not important.

HOTEL CLASSIFICATIONS:

Deluxe: An excellent hotel, rooms with private bath, a/c, more than one restaurant serving very good food, swimming pool, bars, lounges, room service, and all the amenities of a four or five-star international hotel.

First Class: A very comfortable hotel, rooms with private bath, a/c, at least one restaurant, bar, most have a swimming pools.

Tourist Class: Comfortable hotel with simple rooms with private bath, most with a/c, restaurant, bar, and may have a swimming pool.

LODGE AND TENTED CAMP CLASSIFICATIONS:

Class A: Deluxe lodge or tented camp, excellent food and service, large nicely appointed rooms or tents with private bath, comfortable beds and tasteful decor; lodges may have a/c.

Class B: Very comfortable lodge (may have a/c) or camp, rooms in lodges with private bath, large tents, most with private bathrooms, very good food and service, many with swimming pools.

Class C: Simple lodge (with private bathroom) or tented camp (may have private bathroom), good food and service.

Class D: Basic lodge or tented camp, lodges may have private bathrooms, tents without bathrooms, or a Class C structure with poor food, service, or other problems such as water shortages (for bathing).

Class F: Very basic lodge or tented camp without private bathrooms, often self-service (no restaurant).

TEN TOP GAME VIEWING COUNTRIES

BOTSWANA

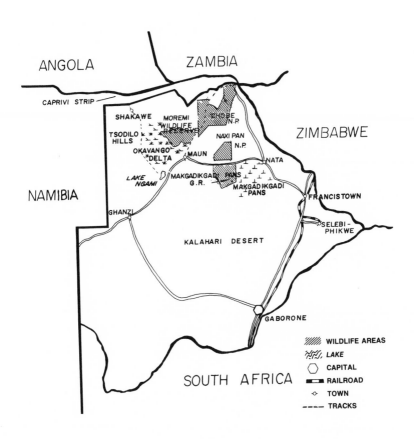

FACTS AT A GLANCE

Area: 224,606 square miles
Approximate size: Texas
Population: 1.2 million (1987 est.)
Capital: Gaborone (pop. about 60,000)
Languages: Official: English; Setswana is
                    the national language.

The Cry of the Kalahari and the hilarious feature film "The God's Must Be Crazy" have assisted Botswana in gaining international recognition as a top safari destination.

More than 4/5ths of the country is covered by the Kalahari sands, scrub savannah and grasslands. The land is basically flat with a mean elevation of 3280 feet. Over 85% of the population is concentrated near the better water resources in the eastern part of the country.

The "Pula" is Botswana's unit of currency and the Setswana word for rain which is so critical to this country's wealth and survival. The rainy season is October-April with the heaviest rains from December-January. Winter brings almost cloudless skies. Average January (summer) temperatures range from a maximum of 92° F to a minimum of 64° F. Average July (winter) temperatures range from a maximum of 72° F to a minimum of 42° F.

The San, Basarwa, or Bushmen were the first inhabitants of the area, and may have come to Southern Africa 30,000 years ago. Most of the estimated 60,000 Bushmen live in what is now Botswana and Namibia. Their language uses "clicking" sounds, distinguishing it from Bantu and most other languages in the world.

Traditionally Bushmen have been nomadic hunter-gatherers, but today only a few thousand live this kind of existence in the Kalahari. Men hunt with poisoned arrows and spears while women use sticks to dig up roots and gather other food for the group.

Bushmen are unique in that they distribute wealth equally among the members of the group, share in the day-to-day aspects of life, and believe they are not superior to their environment and must live in harmony with it.

The Sotho-Tswana group of people comprise over half of the country's population, and speak the Setswana language. The Batswana prefer to live in large, densely populated villages. Cattle are the most important sign of wealth and prestige. Ancestor worship was the chief form of religion until missionaries arrived in 1816 and converted large numbers of Batswana to Christianity.

Bechuanaland became a protectorate of the British Empire September 30, 1885, and became independent Botswana on September 30, 1966.

Today, very few of the people dress in their traditional costume except for special celebrations. However, for many Batswana, tribal customs are still important in day-to-day life. English is spoken by most of the people, and especially by the youth.

Botswana is a multi-party democracy, and one of the most economically successful and politically stable countries on the continent. Minerals are the country's most important foreign exchange. Diamonds and copper-nickel matte comprise over 80% of Botswana's total exports. Meanwhile, there are three times as many cattle in Botswana as people, and cattle are the second most important exchange earner.

WILDLIFE AND WILDLIFE AREAS

Botswana is one of gameviewing's best kept secrets. National parks and reserves cover 17% of the country's area — one of the highest percentages of any country in the world.

Chobe National Park and Moremi Wildlife Reserve rank as two of the best wildlife areas on the continent and fall easily within the top 10. The Okavango Delta is the largest inland delta in the world. This "water in the desert" phenomenon has created a unique and fascinating ecosystem well worth exploring.

The Wildlife Department runs the parks. Driving in the parks is not allowed at night. Camping is allowed at designated spots.

Calving season throughout the country is November-February during the rainy season. Fishing is excellent in the Okavango Delta, Moremi Wildlife Reserve, and the Chobe River May-August. Species include tiger fish, bream and barbel.

Northern Botswana contains the country's three most

important wildlife attractions: Chobe National Park, Moremi Wildlife Reserve, and the Okavango Delta. Other attractions include Nxai Pan National Park and Makgadikgadi Pans Game Reserve.

Generally speaking, gameviewing and bird watching for the Okavango Delta, Chobe and Moremi is best in the dry, cool winter season (May-September) and poorest (November-February) during the hot, rainy season; Nxai and Makgadikgadi are best in the wet summer season (December-April) and poorest (May-November). Many private camps close January-February.

THE NORTH

MAUN

A dusty little town situated at the southeastern tip of the Okavango Delta, Maun is the safari center of the country's most important tourist region. Many travelers fly into Maun and hire vehicles or join a safari.

ACCOMMODATION — TOURIST CLASS • Riley's Hotel is the best place to stay in Maun; bathrooms en suite, a/c, popular bar and good restaurant. • Island Camp, out of town on the river.

CAMPING: • Sitatunga, quiet tented camp and camping sites 9 miles southwest of Maun. Bar, prepared meals, crocodile farm.

THE OKAVANGO DELTA

The Okavango, the largest inland delta in the world, covers over 4,015 square miles and is in itself a unique and fascinating ecosystem. Instead of finding its way to the ocean as most rivers do, the Okavango River fans out into a vast system of waterways separated by innumerable islands to eventually disappear into the Kalahari sands.

The Okavango, an ornithologist's and botanist's dream come true, is beautifully presented in Peter Johnson & Anthony Bannister's book, *Okavango: Sea of Land, Land of Water* (Struik Publishers).

Game viewing for the larger land mammal species should not be your main reason for visiting the Okavango. Big game exists in the delta but is less commonly seen than in Chobe. The main reason for visiting the Okavango should be to

Mokoro

explore the wonder of this inland delta, to enjoy the pri-
mordial silence, the flora, the birdlife, hippo, crocs, excellent
fishing, and the occasional large land mammal.

Game viewing is actually quite good on Chief's Island and
the outlying areas of the delta during the cooler months when
the water is high. Crocodiles are most heavily concentrated in
the larger waterways and in the northern part of the delta
where there is permanent deep water. Mother nature must
have smiled on this region, for the delta waters are highest
during the dry season, since it takes six months for the rainy
season flood waters to travel from their source in the Angolan
highlands to the delta.

The best way to experience the Okavango is to fly to one of
the camps deep in the delta and rent a mokoro (dug out
canoe) with guide or a houseboat. A 12 mile buffalo fence has
been constructed to keep cattle from the swamp, so little game
is found on the Maun (southern) side of the fence.

Flying into the swamps is an adventure in itself. Game can be easily spotted and photographed from the air, gaining a good overall perspective of the swamp. Most charter flights have weight limits of 22 pounds per person, so bring only what you need.

Excursions using mokoros, canoes or small motor boats range in length from a few hours to 10 days or more. Canoes are larger and therefore a little more comfortable, but mokoros harmonize better with the natural surroundings. Motoring allows you to cover more area in a limited time and may be best for people with specific interests (i.e. fishing). Camp is usually made on sandbanks. A guide is strongly recommended; it is easy to get lost in this myriad of waterways and islands. Trips are available through the camps and are included in a number of international tour operator packages.

Traveling by mokoro allows you to become a part of the environment. Sitting inches from the water-line, thoughts of angry hippos or hungry crocodiles overturning your boat cross your mind but soon pass away with assurances from your guide and the peacefulness of this pristine environment.

Silence is broken only by the Ngashi (boatman's pole) penetrating and leaving the water, by the cries of countless birds, and the movement of mostly unseen game along the Delta's banks. Tiny white bell frogs chime to some unknown melody. Sunsets with rosy-pink clouds reflected in the waters are too beautiful for words. Life slows to a regenerative pace. This relaxed form of adventure and exploration is difficult to match anywhere in the world.

On a hot day the sundowner cruise is especially welcome. The boat is often tied to reeds and everyone jumps in! Swimming is quite safe as long as you stay close to your guide and keep away from deep areas which crocodiles prefer.

On numerous occasions our guide waved a fish in the air and called to a fish eagle perched high in a tree over a half-mile away, then tossed the fish into the water about 30 feet from the boat. Like magic, the eagle flew down at full speed and plucked the fish from the water. You have to be fast with a camera to catch that on film!

One day we spotted four young tsessebe standing alone under a tree. We approached within about 50 feet of them, but they still held their ground. Shortly afterwards a herd of adult tsessebe approached within about 100 feet and stopped. The two groups began communicating, using clicking sounds. A female ran from the adult herd to the juveniles, and then ran off into the bush with what we guessed was her calf. Then, a second female did the same thing, followed by two other females which took away the last two juveniles.

Calling the Okavango a "swamp" is a misnomer, since the waters are very clear. Many people drink directly from the delta waters. Apparently the desert sands filter out most of the impurities. There is very little bilharzia in the area.

The islands in the delta are thought to have been made over the eons by termite mounds, and because of their cement-like qualities are presently used to build airstrips and elevated paths in the camps. Diamond prospectors inspect termite mounds closely, since dirt is brought up from quite a depth, thus providing them with easily accessible core samples.

ACCOMMODATION — CLASS A: • Camp Okavango, expensive deluxe tented camp in the eastern delta. • Xugana Game Lodge, on the edge of a lagoon, eight deluxe double tents and the Sitatunga Houseboat which sleeps six. • Shinde Island Camp, six deluxe double tents.

CLASS B: • Xaxaba, 10 attractive reed-thatched huts with private facilities in the south-central delta. Knowledgeable and friendly staff, excellent food and service, sundowner cruises are included.

CLASS C: • Itchau Camp, basic permanent tented camp in the central delta with separate facilities.

MOREMI WILDLIFE RESERVE

Moremi is the most diversified of all the parks in terms of wildlife and scenery, and many people feel it is the most beautiful. Located in the northeastern part of the Okavango Delta, Moremi contains over 1160 square miles of permanent swamps, islands, flood plains, forests and dry land.

In the flood plains reedbuck, waterbuck, lechwe, tsessebe, ostrich, sable and roan antelope, crocodile, hippo and otter can be found. In the riparian forest you may spot elephant, kudu, giraffe, impala, buffalo, zebra and occasionally rhino, along with such predators as lion, leopard, wild dog, ratel, brown and spotted hyena. Rarer species include pangolin, bat-

Spotted Hyena

Porcupine

eared fox, porcupine, hedgehog, black-backed and striped jackals.

Elephant and buffalo are the only large animals that migrate. During the rainy season (October-April) they move northwards to the area between Moremi and the Kwando-Linyati River systems. Other wildlife may move to the periphery of, or just outside, the reserve.

Moremi is an ornithologist's delight. Fish eagles, kingfishers and bee-eaters abound. Other species include parrots, shrikes, egrets, jacanas, pelicans, hornbills, cranes, herons, and storks.

Moremi is open year-round; however some areas may be temporarily closed due to heavy rains or floods. Four-wheel drive vehicles are necessary. The South Gate is about 62 miles north of Maun.

ACCOMMODATION — CLASS A: The following private camps and lodges are located just outside of the reserve: • Tsaro Safari Camp, on the eastern edge of the delta on the Khwai River flats in the delta, expensive luxury camp, swimming pool. • Mombo, on the western side of Chief's Island. • Khwai River Lodge, borders Moremi's northern gate, brick and thatch bandas. • San-Ta-Wani Safari Lodge near Moremi's south gate, brick and thatched lodge. • Camp Moremi, tented camp just north of Moremi. • Machaba Camp, on the Khwai River.

CAMPING: Campsites are available in the reserve. Beware of lions.

CHOBE NATIONAL PARK

Famous for its large herds of elephant, Chobe National Park covers about 30,300 square miles, and is Botswana's best park for seeing big game. The park is situated only about 50 miles from Victoria Falls in Zimbabwe with the Chobe River forming its northern and northwestern boundaries. Across the river is Namibia's Caprivi Strip. Birdlife is prolific, especially in the riverine areas.

The four main regions of the park are Serondela in the northeast near Kasane, the Corridor around Ngwezumba and Nogatsaa, the Linyati Swamps in the northwest, and the Savuti in the west.

The Serondela region is famous for its huge elephant and buffalo populations numbering in the thousands. The elephant are the most vocal and active I've encountered on the continent — constantly trumpeting, making mock charges, and sometimes sparing with each other. Great entertainment!

Elephant

Along the Chobe River between the Chobe Game Lodge and the village of Kasane you are likely to see numerous hippo, lechwe, waterbuck, warthog, and guinea fowl. Driving from the lodge towards Serondela Camp you can usually see giraffe, impala, zebra, and occasionally kudu and bushbuck. We also spotted white rhino, red lechwe, warthog, lion, hammerkop, lilac-breasted roller, grey lourie, white-necked and white-backed vultures.

The hot and dry Corridor (Ngwezumba to Nogatsaa) is the only area in the country where oribi is found. Prevalent species include giraffe, eland, and roan and sable antelope.

The Linyati Swamps are predominately papyrus marsh and are home to many crocodiles, hippo, sitatunga, and lechwe, along with some elephant and buffalo.

Up until several years ago the Savuti afforded fabulous gameviewing opportunities, containing vast populations of elephant, zebra, buffalo, eland, kudu, roan, sable, waterbuck, tsessebe, wildebeest, impala, and many other members of the family of ungulates (hoofed mammals). The predator population was correspondingly tremendous and the Savuti was famous for its lions which occasionally are seen wearing radio tracking collars. Other predators included leopard, cheetah, wild dog, hyena, and jackal. However, because of a 10-year drought there is very little game to be seen in the area as of this writing. After good rains are reported in the area the wildlife will begin to return.

ACCOMMODATION — CLASS A: • Chobe Game Lodge, on the Chobe River, beautifully decorated Moorish style lodge, swimming pool, bar, excellent dining and service, sundowner cruises, game-drives. • Savuti South, a luxury tented camp in the Savuti.

CLASS B: • Lloyd's Camp, on the banks of the Savuti River.

CAMPING: Public campsites are situated at Serondela, Tjinga and Savuti, and self-catered chalets are located at Nogatsaa.

KASANE

Kasane is a small town a few miles north of Chobe National Park. Kasane Enterprises has a small shop of quality souvenirs.

ACCOMMODATION — CLASS A: • Chobe Chilwero Camp, wooden chalets overlooking Chobe National Park.

CAMPING: • Chobe Safari Lodge, rondavels and camping.

OTHER NORTHERN ATTRACTIONS

Nxai Pan National Park is a fossil lake bed with a huge giraffe population, located north of the Maun-Nata road. Other wildlife includes gemsbok, eland, and many predators.

Makgadikgadi Pans Game Reserve includes a portion of the 4600 square mile Makgadikgadi Pans which are the size of Portugal. The pans are nearly devoid of human habitation, giving one the feeling of truly being alone. Once one of the world's largest prehistoric lakes, the Makgadikgadi Pans are salt plains covered with grasslands and occasional baobab and palm trees.

Large herds of wildebeest, zebra, springbok and gemsbok and thousands of flamingos can usually be seen December-March.

Thousands of Bushmen paintings are scattered through the rocky outcrops of **Tsodilo Hills**, one of the last places in Botswana where Bushmen can be fairly easily found. Access is by a flight across the delta from Maun or a rough day's ride by vehicle. Please do not drink anything in the presence of Bushmen — water is scarce.

Eighty percent of the country is covered in Kalahari sands but only 10% of the population lives on them. The **Kalahari Desert** is not a barren desert of rolling dunes as one might imagine. It has scattered grasslands, bush, shrub and tree savannah, dry river beds, and occasional rocky outcrops.

The Kalahari has an abundance of wildebeest, hartebeest, springbok, gemsbok, ostrich, eland and giraffe. Bushmen are very difficult to find in the Kalahari, so seeing them should be considered a bonus.

Flamingos

THE SOUTH

GABORONE

Gaborone is the capital of Botswana. In the center of town is the main shopping center — the Mall. Points of interest include the National Museum.

ACCOMMODATION — FIRST CLASS: • The President Hotel, attractive, very comfortable, centrally located, a/c, excellent dining, friendly staff. • The Gaborone Sun Hotel, on the outskirts of the city, a/c, swimming pool, two restaurants, casino, resident band and cabaret.

KENYA

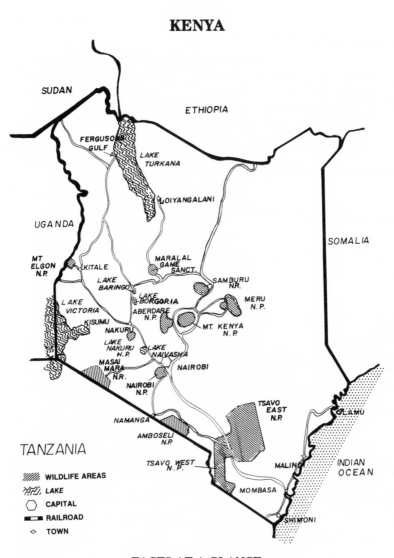

FACTS AT A GLANCE

Area:	224,960 square miles
Approximate size:	Oregon
Population:	20 million (1987 est.)
Capital:	Nairobi (pop. est. 1.4 million)
Languages:	Official: Kiswahili and English

The word **safari** is Swahili for "travel," and Kenya is where it all began. Great historical figures like Theodore Roosevelt and Ernest Hemingway immortalized this country. Kenya is now the most popular of the safari countries, with over 600,000 visitors per year. Visitors to Kenya can enjoy game viewing, birdwatching, mountaineering, SCUBA diving, fresh water and deepsea fishing, and numerous other activities.

Kenya is well-known for the magnificent Serengeti migration of nearly two million wildebeest and zebra and for the colorful Masai, Samburu and other tribes that contribute so much to making this a top safari destination.

The eastern and northern regions of the country are arid. Most of the population and economic production is in the south which is characterized by a plateau ranging in altitude from 3,000-10,000 feet sloping down to Lake Victoria in the west and a coastal strip to the east.

Kenya has one of the most diversely majestic landscapes on the continent. The Great Rift Valley is more breathtakingly dramatic here than anywhere else in Africa, with the steep walled valley floor dropping as much as 2000-3000 feet from the surrounding countryside.

The country has the highest population growth rate in the world (4.1%), with women having an average of eight children in their lifetimes. Over half the country is Christian, about 25% indigenous beliefs, and 6% Muslim concentrated along the coast. The Masai are found mainly to the west and south of Nairobi, the Kikuyu in the highlands around Nairobi and the Samburu in the North.

Bantu and Nilotic peoples moved into the area before Arab traders arrived on the Kenyan coast by the first century A.D. The Swahili language was created out of a mixture of Bantu and Arabic and became the universal trading language. The Portuguese arrived in 1498 and took command of the coast, followed by the Omani in the 1600's and the British in the late 19th century. Kenya gained its independence within the Commonwealth from Britain on December 12, 1963. Key foreign exchange earners are coffee and tea, and tourism.

WILDLIFE AND WILDLIFE AREAS

Kenya is one of the best countries on the continent for game viewing. Its only drawback is that it is too popular. Many of the well-known parks are very crowded, so don't expect to be out there in the more popular parks completely on your own.

Unlike many African countries, game is widespread outside of the national parks and reserves as well as within, probably because of the ban on hunting game. Many mobile tented camp safari operators spend a good portion of their time in uncrowded areas outside the parks that are also rich in game.

In general, game viewing is best during the dry seasons

January to mid-April and July-October. Game is easiest to spot in the Masai Mara, Amboseli and Nairobi National Park, which have great wide-open plains.

The country is an ornithologist's paradise with over 650 species of birds recorded within its borders. Greater and Lesser flamingos migrate along the Rift Valley and prefer the alkaline lakes of Magadi, Elmenteita, Nakuru, Borgoria and Turkana. Lakes Naivasha and Baringo are fresh-water lakes. Birdwatching is good year-round.

The central government is in charge of the national parks while local governing bodies are in charge of the reserves. The Masai Mara is the best park in Kenya for game viewing, and should, if all possible, be included in one's itinerary unless you will be touring the Serengeti National Park in Tanzania at the times of the year when wildlife is more concentrated in the Serengeti National Park and there is no time to also include the Masai Mara.

Flying safaris are available to many of the parks and reserves. Camel safaris are operated in the north where guests walk down dry river beds or ride these "ships of the desert."

THE SOUTH

NAIROBI

"Nairobi" in the Masai language means "place of cool waters," and is one of my two favorite cities on the continent for long-term stays. The pioneer atmosphere coupled with the availability of international-class accommodation and most western goods and services make living and visiting here an enjoyable adventure.

The National Museum of Nairobi features the Leakey family's paleoanthropological discoveries, botanical drawings of Joy Adamson, and taxidermy displays of wild animals that are good to study to help you identify the live game while on safari. Across from the museum is the Snake Park, exhibiting over 200 species of the well-loved reptilian family. The Municipal Market in the center of town on Market Street sells produce and curios (be sure to bargain). The Railroad Museum will be of interest to railroad enthusiasts. The Phoenix Players is a theatre featuring very talented actors.

One of the more popular dining and dancing spots is the Carnivore, famous for its beef and game meat. The Horseman, located in the suburb of Karen, is also excellent. The Tamarind is known for excellent seafood. The Thorn Tree Cafe is renowned meeting place for travelers on safari who leave messages on a bulletin board; it is a key center of communication for people on the move and the best spot in town for people-watching.

ACCOMMODATION — LUXURY: • Hilton International, centrally located, swimming pool, restaurants, shops. • Norfolk Hotel, a landmark in Nairobi, traditional safari atmosphere, swimming pool, open-air bar especially popular on Friday nights. • Nairobi Safari Club is a new modern hotel near the university. • Inter-Continental Hotel, near the center of town.

FIRST CLASS: New Stanley.

TOURIST CLASS: Six Eighty Hotel.

NAIROBI ENVIRONS

Nairobi National Park is only eight miles south of Nairobi and sporadically has an abundance of game (depending on the weather) including rhino (on first visit we saw three), lion,

Giraffe

cheetah, hippo and a variety of antelope — a bit of everything but elephants.

There is something very strange about being in the midst of wild game and still within sight of a city's skyline. The animal orphanage (a small zoo) near the main park entrance cares for hurt, sick or stray animals. The side of the park facing Nairobi is fenced.

Other attractions include the **Bomas of Kenya** which features daily performances of ethnic dances and 16 varying styles of Kenyan homesteads. At the **Giraffe Centre** guests can feed the Rothschild giraffes from an elevated platform and learn more about them. **Mayer's Ranch**, situated 30 miles from Nairobi in the Rift Valley, presents traditional Masai moran (warrior) dances and has a Masai manyata (village). The home of **Karen Blixen** is now a museum and is interesting to visit.

AMBOSELI NATIONAL PARK

The real attraction of this park is the spectacular backdrop Mt. Kilimanjaro. Also, rhino are probably easier to locate here than in any other park in Kenya.

This 146 square mile park is probably the most crowded in the country, and a large portion of it has been turned into a dust-bowl. On the other hand, elephant, lion and giraffe are easily found, and watching and photographing them as they pass in front of majestic Mt. Kilimanjaro is one of the most treasured sites on the continent.

From Nairobi drive south across the Athi Plains inhabited by the Masai. One enters the park on a badly corrugated road from Namanga and passes Lake Amboseli, bone dry except in the rainy seasons, then eastward across sparsely vegetated chalk flats to Ol Tukai.

The barren landscape turns refreshingly green in the center of the park as springs and swamps, fed by an underground run off from the overshadowing Mt. Kilimanjaro, provide water for grasslands and acacia woodlands which attract an abundance of game, giving life to an otherwise parched land. Large herds of elephant and buffalo are often seen around the swamps, especially at Enkongo Narok where photos of animals in the foreground and Mt. Kilimanjaro in the background can be

Vervet Monkey

most easily obtained. Early mornings are best before Kilimanjaro is covered in clouds. Observation Hill is a good location for
spotting lion and to get an overview of the park.

One has a pretty good chance of spotting lion, cheetah,
giraffe, and impala. Wild dog, aardwolf, oryx and gerenuk are
less likely to be seen. Over 420 species of birds have been
recorded. Game viewing is best January-March (also best views
of Kilimanjaro) and July-October.

ACCOMMODATION — Amboseli Lodge, Kilimanjaro Safari
Lodge and park headquarters are located at Ol Tukai in the
center of the park.

CLASS B: • Amboseli Lodge, rustic, swimming pool. • Amboseli
Serena Lodge, modern, swimming pool, located in the south of
the park.

CLASS C: Kilimanjaro Safari Lodge, swimming pool.

CAMPING: Outside the park on Masai land 4 miles past
Observation Hill. Bring your own water.

TSAVO WEST NATIONAL PARK

Half way between Nairobi and Mombasa lies Tsavo West and
East National Parks, which together total 8,217 square miles.
Large herds of over 200 elephant, with a total of 20,000 in
Tsavo West and East combined, over 60 species of mammals
and 400 species of birds have been recorded. Also present are
lion, caracal, giraffe, zebra and a variety of antelope.

Tsavo West is predominately extensive semi-arid plains
broken by occasional granite outcrops. The Ngulia Mountains
with peaks rising to nearly 6000 feet dominate the northern
region of the park.

Mzima Springs, located just south of Kilaguni Lodge, is the
park's premier attraction. From an underwater viewing platform visitors may be lucky enough to watch hippos swim about
the clear waters with grace and ease. Crocs and numerous
species of fish can also be seen. The best viewing is early in the
morning before many visitors have arrived.

ACCOMMODATION — CLASS A: Taita Hills Lodge and Salt
Lick Lodge are situated between the southern extensions of
Tsavo East and West Parks. • Salt Lick Lodge, built on stilts to
enhance viewing of wildlife visiting the salt lick. • Taita Hills

Lodge.
CLASS B: • Kilaguni, in north central region of the park, comfortable, floodlit waterhole, swimming pool. • Ngulia Lodge, flood-lit waterhole.
CAMPING: Numerous sites available.

TSAVO EAST NATIONAL PARK

Tsavo East is mostly arid bush dotted with rocky outcrops traversed by seasonal rivers lined with riverine forest. Tsavo East is generally hotter, dryer, and lies at a lower altitude (about 1,000 feet) than its western counterpart. The 3,000 square mile section south of the Galana River is the main region open to the public.

East Tsavo's only permanent waterhole is at Aruba Dam, and the drive from Voi makes for a good game run. Just north of the dam is an isolated hill, Mudanda Rock, another good spot for game. The scenic drive along the Galana River often produces sightings of hippos and crocs. Walking safaris are operated along the Tsavo River.
ACCOMMODATION — CLASS C • Voi Safari Lodge, in the hills above the town of Voi, two waterholes and a photographic hide. • Crocodile Camp, full service camp on the Galana River just outside Sala Gate on the park's eastern boundary.

MASAI MARA NATIONAL RESERVE

This is the finest reserve in Kenya. All the big game is here: elephant, lion, leopard, cheetah and buffalo are prevalent, along with a few rhino. Other commonly sighted species include zebra, wildebeest, Thomson's gazelle, and giraffe. This is the only place in Kenya where topi are common.

The Masai Mara, a northern extension of the Serengeti Plains, is located southwest of Nairobi and covers 198 square miles of the total 692 square mile reserve of open plains, acacia woodlands, and riverine forest along the banks on the Mara and Talek Rivers which are home for many hippos, crocs and water fowl.

One of the best places to look for game is in the western part of the reserve bounded by the Siria Escarpment on the west, the Tanzanian border to the south and the Mara River to

Thomson's Gazelle

the east. A multitude of savannah animals can be found on these open grasslands.

The best time to visit is during the migration from July to mid-September when great herds of wildebeest (1.4 million) and zebra (400,000) reside in the area before returning to Tanzania. At this time prides of 40 or more lion may be seen. From the Serengeti of Tanzania, the main migration moves towards Lake Victoria, then north across the Mara River into Kenya in search of grass, returning to Tanzania in October/November.

ACCOMMODATION IN THE RESERVE — CLASS A: • Governor's Camp and Little Governor's Camp, in the northwest of the park, deluxe tented camps in the finest tradition. Frequented by celebrities and royalty, superb cuisine and service, inexplicably magic atmosphere, exciting hot-air balloon excursions. • Mara Intrepids Club, deluxe tented camp, swimming

pool, balloon safaris, situated on the Talek River. • Sarova Mara Camp. • Mara Serena Lodge, comfortable rooms, swimming pool, restaurant.
CLASS B: • Keekorok, old-style colonial lodge, rooms with private facilities, balloon safaris.
ACCOMMODATION ON THE PERIPHERY OF THE RESERVE — CLASS B: • Kichwa Tembo Camp, tented camp, dining room and lounge in a nearby building. Good food.
CLASS C: • Cottar's Masai Mara Camp. Night safaris.
CAMPING: Sites are outside the park along the Talek River.

THE WEST

MT. ELGON NATIONAL PARK

Seldomly visited, this 65 square mile park is a huge, extinct volcano shared with Uganda, and at 14,178 feet is the second highest mountain in Kenya. Mt. Elgon also has the giant Afro-alpine flora found on Mts. Kenya and Kilimanjaro.

The forests are often so thick that a full-grown elephant could be standing 20 feet from the road and not be seen. Buffalo, waterbuck, and bushbuck are more likely to be spotted.

Kitum and Makingeny caves are unique in having a good portion of their sizes created by elephants. Small herds enter the caves near dusk to spend several hours in complete darkness mining salts with their tusks. Thousands of bats keep the elephants company. Makingeny is the largest, but Kitum is more frequently visited by elephants. During our visit elephant droppings were everywhere, foreshadowing the real possibility of their sources being inside.

To explore the caves be sure to bring two or more strong flashlights. Access to the park is difficult in the rainy season when four-wheel drive vehicles are recommended.
ACCOMMODATION — CLASS C: Mount Elgon Lodge, situated just outside the park entrance.
CAMPING: Sites available in the park.

OTHER ATTRACTIONS

Kisumu, located on the shores of **Lake Victoria**, is the third largest city in Kenya with a population over 115,000. The

Sunset Hotel provides tourist class accommodation in comfortable air-conditioned rooms.

THE MOUNT KENYA CIRCUIT

ABERDARE NATIONAL PARK

This 300 square mile park of luxuriant forest includes much of the Aberdare (renamed Nyandarua) Range of mountains. Guests of two famous tree hotels, Treetops and the Ark, are entertained by a variety of wildlife visiting their waterholes and salt licks.

The park can be divided into two sections by altitude. A high plateau of undulating moorlands with tussock grasses and giant heather lies between Ol Doinyo Lasatima (13,120 ft.) and Kinangop (12,816 ft). Lion, hyena, buffalo, elephant, eland, reedbuck, suni, black serval cat, bush pig and very rarely, the nocturnal bongo can be seen, along with excellent views of Mt. Kenya and the Rift Valley.

On the eastern slopes below lies the forested hills and valleys of the Salient, home to rhino, leopard, forest elephant, buffalo, waterbuck, bushbuck, giant forest hog, and black and white colobus monkey.

ACCOMMODATION — CLASS C: • The Ark, a "tree hotel" overlooking waterhole, rooms without facilities, suites with facilities, glass-enclosed main viewing lounge, outside veranda on each level, floodlit for all-night game viewing. • Treetops, the first of the "tree hotels" (on stilts,) older and more rustic than the Ark.

CAMPING: Only by special permission of the warden.

MOUNT KENYA NATIONAL PARK

Kenya's highest mountain and the second highest on the continent, Mount Kenya lies just below the equator, yet has several permanent glaciers.

Mount Kenya's two highest peaks, Batian (17,058 ft.) and Nelion (17,023 ft.), are accessible by 25 routes and should be attempted only by experienced rock climbers. Point Lenana (16,355 ft.) is a non-technical climb accessible to hikers in good condition, and is best climbed in the dry seasons. January-February is the best time to go when views are the clearest and temperatures are warmer on top. Vegetation changes are similar to those described for the Ruwenzori Mountains (see Zaire) and Mt. Kilimanjaro (see Tanzania).

Rock climbing routes on the south side of the mountain are in best condition from late December to mid-March, while routes on the north side are best climbed from late June to mid-October. Ice routes are best attempted during the same periods but on opposite sides of the mountain.

Climbers should be on the lookout for buffalo and forest elephant, although rarely seen. Other wildlife that may be encountered includes leopard, duiker, bushbuck, giant forest hog, and colobus monkeys.

The climb to Point Lenana normally takes three days up and one or two down. The first night is often spent at Naro Moru Lodge, or better yet, at the Met Station (10,000 ft.) to assist altitude acclimatization. Accommodation en route is in huts, tented camps or your own tent.

The Naro Moru route is via Teleki Hut (13,630 ft.), Mackinder's Camp (14,200 ft.), Austrian Hut (15,714 ft.) from which the ascent to Point Lenana is usually attempted, and for technical climbers, Howell Hut (17,020 ft.) on the summit of Nelion, which sleeps two. The view from Point Lenana was the clearest and one of the most magnificent panoramas I've seen from any mountain.

There is a five-day or so circuit route around Mt. Kenya with accommodation in basic huts spaced an easy day's walk apart.

Our getting to Mt. Kenya proved almost as difficult as the climb itself. My partner and I loaded our backpacks on the handlebars of two motorcycles and began a pleasant drive from the town of Nakuru on a beautiful sunny day. Soon it began to rain and the back roads turned to mud so slick that my bike slipped right out from under me, and I crashed on the rock-strewn road.

The mud became too deep to ride, and we had to push the bikes for miles. We had planned to camp at the Met Station that evening to acclimatize, but darkness overcame us even before we reached the Naro Moru Lodge. As I limped into the lodge covered from head to toe with mud, I thought "What a way to begin a climbing expedition!"

Because climbers can ascend to high altitudes very quickly,

Mount Kenya claims more than half of the world's deaths from pulmonary edema. My climbing partner had symptoms of pulmonary edema after reaching Austrian Hut (15,715 ft.), and we had to abandon our attempt of Batian Peak and return to lower altitudes. Therefore, a slow, sensible approach is recommended.

The world's highest altitude SCUBA diving record was shattered at Two Tarn Lake (14,720 ft.), one of the more than 30 lakes on the mountain. The previous record of 12,500 feet was set at Lake Titicaca in Bolivia. In addition, climbers are occasionally seen ice skating on the Curling Pond, below the Lewis Glacier.

Lone climbers are usually not allowed to enter the park. The Mountain Club of Kenya (Wilson Airport, P.O. Box 45741, Nairobi; tel: 501747) has meetings at the MCK Clubhouse every Tuesday night around 7:30 pm; this is a good place to look for partners.

Huts and camping sites may be booked at Naro Moru River

Lioness and Cub

Lodge. Guides and porters may also be booked at the lodge or at the park gate. Tour operators can handle all details. Members of the Mountain Club of Kenya can use the club's huts at a discount. Little if any equipment is available in Kenya, so bring whatever you need.

ACCOMMODATION — CLASS A: • The Mount Kenya Safari Club, most famous lodge in all of East Africa, built by actor William Holden. Spacious gardens are frequented by many species of exotic birds, swimming pool, 9-hole golf course, exquisite cuisine, very comfortable rooms, suites and luxury cottages with fireplaces. Located on the slopes of Mt. Kenya outside of the national park near Nanyuki.

CLASS C: • Naro Moru River Lodge, located below the park, fullboard chalets, rustic self-service cabins, restaurant and bar. Climbing safaris arranged some equipment (sleeping bags, boots, etc.) available for hire. Four-wheel drive vehicles for hire to transport guests to the park entrance. • Mountain Lodge, a "tree hotel" set in a forest outside the park boundary.

CAMPING: • At the Naro Moru Lodge and in the park.

MERU NATIONAL PARK

Meru is best known for where Elsa, the lioness of Joy Adamson's *Born Free*, was rehabilitated to the wild. This 300 square mile park is located east of Mt. Kenya, 220 miles from Nairobi.

The swamps are host to most of Meru's 5,000 buffalo, sometimes seen in herds of more than 200, and a number of elephant. Oryx, eland, reticulated giraffe and Grevy's zebra are

plentiful on the plains, where lion are also most likely to be seen. Lesser kudu, gerenuk and cheetah can be found, along with hippos and crocs within the Tana River. Rhino are most likely to be seen in the west central region of the park. Leopard are also prevalent, and over 300 species of birds have been recorded.

ACCOMMODATION — CLASS C: • Meru Mulika Lodge.

CAMPING: Sites available. Contact the Warden, P.O. Box 162, Nairobi.

UP THE RIFT VALLEY

Lake Naivasha, about an hour's drive (55 miles) northwest of Nairobi, is a fresh-water lake prolific in birdlife and a favorite spot for picnics and watersports for Nairobi residents. Crescent Island is a bird sanctuary and is also host to numerous antelope and a few camels. Boat rides are available.

Accommodation (Class B) is available at the beautifully landscaped Lake Naivasha Hotel which has a swimming pool and serves a special Sunday afternoon tea. Rooms and campsites are available at The Safariland Lodge (Class B), which has a swimming pool and offers horseback riding.

Nakuru National Park encompasses the alkaline lake of the same name and is frequently visited by hundreds of thousands of greater and lesser flamingos. Other wildlife includes rhino, lion, Rothschild giraffe, waterbuck, reedbuck, hippo and baboons, pelicans and cormorants. Located 100 miles northwest of Nairobi on a fair road, the park covers 78 square miles. Accommodation is provided by Lion Hill Lodge (Class B) with bandas and swimming pool and Lake Nakuru Lodge (Class C). Camping sites are available in the park.

Thompson's Falls, located above the Rift Valley between Nanyuki and Nakuru at Nyahururu, is a refreshing place to relax. Thompson's Falls Lodge is a rustic country hotel (Class C).

Lake Borgoria National Reserve, located north of Nakuru, has numerous hot springs and geysers along the lake shore. Thousands of flamingos frequent this alkaline lake, as do greater kudu on the steep slopes of the lake's eastern and southern shores. Fig tree Camp (campsites only) is situated at the south end of the lake.

Lake Baringo is a fresh water lake north of Lake Borgoria and a haven for a colorful and mixed variety of birdlife, and a sporting center for water skiing, fishing and boating.

Island Camp is a very peaceful tented camp (Class B) situated in the center of Lake Baringo. All tents have private facilities. The 6:30 am boat ride along the lake shore is one of the finest birdwatching excursions I've experienced, featuring a great variety of species. Hippos, crocs, fishermen and villages along the shore may also be seen.

THE NORTH

LAKE TURKANA

Called the Jade Sea from its deep green color, Lake Turkana is a huge inland sea surrounded by semi-desert near the Ethiopian border three days of hard driving over rough terrain from Nairobi.

Formerly Lake Rudolf, this huge lake is over 175 miles long and 10 to 30 miles wide, set in a lunar-like landscape of lava rocks, dried up river beds and scattered oases.

The brown Omo River flows from the Ethiopian highlands into the northern part of the lake where the water is fairly fresh, but becomes increasingly saline southward due to intense evaporation. The presence of puffer fish imply that the lake was at one time connected to the Mediterranean Sea by the River Nile.

Because the bitter alkaline waters render the skins of what is one of the continent's largest populations of crocodiles useless for the commercial trade, crocs are not hunted and grow to abnormally large sizes. Although very tempting in such a hot, dry climate, swim at your own risk!

Fishing is a major attraction. Nile perch, the world's largest fresh-water fish, can exceed 400 pounds. Tiger fish, however, put up a more exciting fight. The El Molo tribe, the smallest tribe in Kenya (about 500 members), can be found near Loyangalani.

ACCOMMODATION — CLASS C: • Lake Rudolf Lodge, situated on the western shore of the lake, swimming pool, fishing boats and equipment for hire. • Oasis Lodge, on the south-eastern shore of the lake, two swimming pools, fishing boats

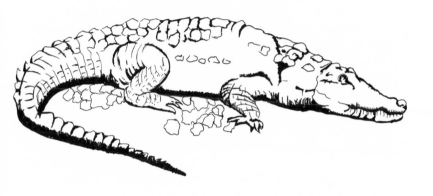

Crocodile

and equipment for hire.

SAMBURU NATIONAL RESERVE

This relatively small 40 square mile park is situated north of Mt. Kenya. This is a park of scrub desert, riverine forest and swamps along the Ewaso Ngiro River. Elephant and lion are plentiful as are Beisa oryx, Somali ostrich, reticulated giraffe, gerenuk, Grevy's zebra and other species adapted to an arid environment. The park is often visited by guests overnighting at the Mt. Kenya Safari Club in Nanyuki.

ACCOMMODATION — CLASS B: • Samburu Lodge, on the banks of the Ewaso Ngiro River, cabins, lodge, tents, good food, croc and leopard baits. • Samburu River Lodge, on the river, new comfortable chalets, croc and leopard baits.

CLASS C: • Buffalo Springs Tented Camp.

CAMPING: Good sites available.

OTHER ATTRACTIONS

Maralal National Sanctuary, located northwest of Samburu, has zebra, buffalo, impala, hyena, and elephant (seasonal) which come to drink at the waterhole adjacent to the Maralal Safari Lodge (Class B). Leopard can often be seen just before sunset from a hide near the lodge. We fortunately saw two of these fascinating creatures during a truly enjoyable visit.

Leopard

THE COAST

MOMBASA

Mombasa is the second largest city in Kenya with a population over 500,000. This island, 307 miles from Nairobi on a paved road, is a blend of the Middle East, Asia and Africa.

The Old Harbor is haven for dhows carrying goods for trade between Arabia and the Indian subcontinent and Africa, especially December-April. Kilindini is the modern harbor and largest port on the east coast of Africa.

Built by the Portuguese in 1593, Fort Jesus now serves as a museum. The Old Town is Muslim and Indian in flavor with winding, narrow streets and alleys too narrow for cars, tall 19th century buildings with hand-carved doors and overhanging balconies, and small shops. The City of Mombasa has no beaches so most international visitors stay on the beautiful beaches to the south or north of the island.

ACCOMMODATION — DELUXE: • Inter-Continental Hotel, new hotel located eight miles north of Mombasa.

TOURIST: • Outrigger Hotel on Mombasa Island.

SOUTH OF MOMBASA

Diani Beach is one of the finest in the country and holds many of the top sea-side resorts. Situated about 20 miles south of Mombasa, the beach is protected by coral reefs. The Nomad restaurant serves excellent seafood.

Deluxe accommodation is provided by Diani Reef Hotel and the Jadini Beach Hotel, both with a/c, swimming pool, dive school, tennis courts. Minilets is a fixed tented camp (Class C) on Tiwi Beach.

Kisite Mpunguti Marine Reserve is situated near the small fishing village of Shimoni (the place of the caves where slaves were held before shipment) near the Tanzanian border far from the mainstream of tourism. Delightful boat excursions to Wasini Island, an ancient Arab settlement across a channel from Shimoni, and snorkeling excursions are available.

The Pemba Channel, just off of Shimoni, is one of the world's finest marlin fishing grounds. The nearest diving equipment rentals are in Diani Beach.

NORTH OF MOMBASA

Once the most popular resort town on the coast, **Malindi** has dropped in popularity at least in part because the nearby Galana River has been muddying the waters along the beaches. There are numerous nightclubs and shops, and the International Bill Fishing competition is held here every January. Malindi is located 75 miles north of Mombasa, two hours by car. The Blue Marlin and Sinbad hotels provide comfortable accommodation (First Class) with swimming pools.

Malindi-Watamu Marine National Reserve encompasses the area south of Malindi to south of Watamu, from 100 feet to three nautical miles offshore, and has very good diving.

Swahili culture has changed little in the past few hundred years on the island of **Lamu.** The only motorized vehicle on the island is owned by a government official, but plenty of donkey carts provide substitutes. Narrow, winding streets and a maze of alleyways add to the timeless atmosphere.

The Lamu Museum has exhibits of Swahili craftwork. Of the over 30 mosques on Lamu, a few are open to visitors. The best beaches are at Shela, a 45 minute walk or short boat ride from Lamu town to the Peponi Beach Hotel. Matondani is a fishing village where dhows, fishing nets and traps are made. Numerous attractions also lie on nearby islands.

The best way to reach the island is to fly; day and overnight excursions from Mombasa and Malindi are available. The road from Malindi is very rough and may be impassable in the rainy season.

Peponi Beach Hotel (First Class) is a pleasant beach resort located about one mile from Lamu town. Petley's Inn (Tourist Class) has been a landmark since the 19th century, with the only bar in town, rustic atmosphere and rooms with private facilities and ceiling fans.

NAMIBIA

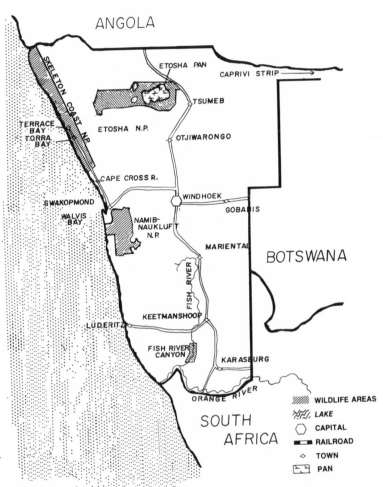

FACTS AT A GLANCE

Area:	321,000 square miles
Approximate size:	Texas + Oklahoma
Population:	1.2 million (1987 est.)
Capital:	Windhoek (pop. est. 100,000)
Languages:	Official: Afrikaans, English, and German

Namibia is one of the most sparsely populated countries in the world. It is famous for its stark beauty and is a geologist's and naturalist's paradise.

Namibia has a subtropical climate. Inland summer (October-April) days are warm to hot with cool nights. Summer is the rainy season, with most rainfall occurring in the north and northeast.

Namibia's population is 86% black, 7% white and 7% colored (of mixed descent). Most people live in the northern part of the country where there is more water. Herero women, colorfully-dressed in red and black, continue to wear conservative, impractical and extremely hot attire fashioned for them by puritanical 19th century missionaries who wished to cover the savage breast.

In 1884 much of the coast became German South West Africa until 1919 when South Africa took control during World War I. The Union of South Africa received a mandate by the League of Nations over the region in 1920; the United Nations retracted the mandate in 1966 and re-named the country Namibia. As of this writing the country still remains under South Africa's control.

Namibia is the world's largest producer of diamonds, has the world's largest uranium mine. Tsumeb is the only known mine which has produced over 100 different minerals.

WILDLIFE AND WILDLIFE AREAS

Winter (May-September) is the best time to visit the game parks in the central and northern regions when days are warm with clear skies and nights are cold.

The rules for Namibia's national parks are the same as for

South African national parks. The parks are well-organized and the facilities clean. For information and reservations contact the Directorate of Nature Conservation (Private Bag 13267, Windhoek 9000; tel: 061-36975; tx: 0908-3180).

THE NORTH

WINDHOEK

Windhoek is the capital, administrative, commercial and educational center of Namibia, situated in the center of the country at 5,600 feet above sea level.

Sights include the three Windhoek castles (Schwerinsburg, Sanderburg and Heinitzburg) built between 1913-1918 and the State Museum at the Alte Feste (Old Fort).

ACCOMMODATION — FIRST CLASS • Kalahari Sands, fine hotel, two restaurants, disco, bar, lounge, swimming pool, roof garden, sauna, fitness center.

TOURIST CLASS • Continental Hotel, rooms with full facilities, two good restaurants, very popular nightclub and disco.

CAMPING: • OASE Caravan Park, nine miles from Windhoek.

ETOSHA NATIONAL PARK

Etosha is Namibia's foremost attraction and one of Africa's greatest parks, covering 8,600 square miles in the northern part of the country and lying 3,300 - 4,900 feet above sea level.

The park is mainly mixed scrub, mopane savannah and dry woodland surrounding the huge Etosha Pan. The pan is a silvery-white shallow depression, dry except during the rainy season. Mirages and dust-devils play across what was once a lake fed by a river that long ago changed course. Along the edge of the pan are springs that attract wildlife during the dry winter season.

The eastern areas of the park experience the most rainfall and have denser bush than the northwestern region which is mainly open grasslands. About 40 waterholes spread out along 500 miles of roads provide many vantage points from which to watch game.

Etosha is famous for its huge elephant population which is most visible August-September in the center of the park. When the rains begin in October-November elephants migrate north to Angola and west to Kaokoland and begin returning in March. Large populations of zebra, blue wildebeest, springbok and gemsbok (oryx) migrate westward from the Namutoni area in October/November to the west and northwest of Okaukuejo Camp where they stay until around March-May. From June-August they migrate eastward again past Okaukuejo and Halali Camps to the Namutoni plains where there is water year-round. The park is totally fenced although this does not always stop the elephants from going where they please.

Lion are commonly seen, and zebra are often sighted way out on the barren pan where lions have no cover from which to launch an attack. Black-faced impala and Damara dikdik are two distinctive species of this area. Rhino prefer the western regions.

During our visit we spotted white rhino, elephant, lion, red hartebeest, greater kudu, giraffe, gemsbok, zebra, blue wildebeest, springbok, black-faced impala, black-backed jackals, honey badger, warthog and mongoose. Other wildlife in the park includes black rhino, brown hyena, spotted hyena, caracal, African wild cat, leopard, cheetah, aardwolf, silver fox, bat-eared fox, eland, roan, sable and grey duiker.

Birdlife is prolific with over 325 species recorded, particularly on the Etosha Pan during the summer rainy season from mid-January to March. However, a diverse range of bird species can be seen year-round. Kites, pelicans, greater and lesser flamingos, and marabou storks migrate seasonally.

Flamingos

Other species commonly sighted include kori bustards, guinea foul, francolins, ostrich, turtle doves, lilac-breasted roller, Namaquwa sandgrouse and crimson-breasted shrike (Namibia's emblem bird).

Roads run along the eastern, southern and western borders of the Etosha pan. There are three camps — Namutoni, Halali, and Okaukuejo. All three camps have lodge accommodations (Class C), caravan and camping sites, swimming pool, restaurant, store, petrol station and landing strip. Rest camps are fenced in for the visitor's protection. In spite of this, jackal roam through the camps and will snatch food left unguarded, even meat right off the grill, but they are no danger to campers. Namutoni is open year-round while Halali and Okaukuejo are open from the second Friday in March to October 31.

Namutoni Camp is situated in the eastern part of the park, seven miles from the Von Lindquist Gate, and features a very attractive fortress built in 1903 and converted to hotel rooms. The area around Namutoni receives more rain than the other region of the park. Eland, kudu and the Damara dikdik, Africa's smallest antelope, are often seen in this area.

Halali Camp is the most modern of the camps, lying halfway between the other two at the foot of a dolomite hill. A good spot to see elephants is at Olifantsbad, a waterhole between Halali and Okaukuejo.

Hartebeest

Okaukuejo Camp lies to the west of the other camps, 11 miles from the Anderson Gate entrance, and has a waterhole adjacent to it that is excellent for wildlife viewing, especially at night when it is floodlit. We witnessed a stand off between a white rhino and two elephants over control of the waterhole. A

Lioness

lioness also came for a drink. The flatulence of the elephants was almost deafening.

From Okaukuejo one can drive north along the eastern edge of the pan to Okondeka and west to the haunted forest, a dense concentration of eerie-looking African Moringa trees. I wouldn't want to walk through this forest at night! On the road from Okaukuejo to Leeubron one passes under a social weaver's nest (birds nest) the size of a car.

THE COAST

The freezing Benguela Current of the Atlantic flows from

Antarctica northwards along the Namibian coastline and meets the hot, dry air of the Namib Desert, forming a thick fog bank which often penetrates inland up to 60 miles. The best time to visit the coast for sunbathing, fishing, and surfing is from December-February; June-July is cold and rainy.

SKELETON COAST NATIONAL PARK

Skeletons of shipwrecks and whales dot the treacherous coast of this park which stretches along the seashore and covers over 2000 square miles of wind-shaped dunes, canyons and jagged peaks of the Namib.

Fog penetrates inland for over 20 miles almost every day and often lingers until the desert sun burns it off at 9:00 — 10:00 am. When the wind blows from the east there is instant sunshine.

The park is divided into southern and northern sections. The southern section is more accessible and lies between the Ugab and Hoanib Rivers. A permit, reservations and payment must be made in advance with the Directorate of Nature Conservation for stays at either Torra Bay or Terrace Bay.

Torra Bay has tents and campsites, and is open only during the December-January holidays. Terrace Bay is open year-round and offers full board and lodging in basic bungalows (Class C) and has a landing strip for light aircraft.

The northern part of the park has been designated as a wilderness area and can only be visited with fly-in safaris run by Louw Schoeman. Louw and his wife Amy know this region better than anyone. Amy is the author of *Skeleton Coast* (Macmillan Publishers), a superb pictorial and factual representation of this fascinating region.

From Windhoek guests are flown to Swakopmund, then northwards some 370 miles to Louw's fully-catered tented camp between Rocky Point and Cape Frio. Daily excursions from camp are made to explore the area.

A walk down the "roaring dunes" will give you the surprise of your life. Suddenly everyone is looking up to spot the B-52 bomber that must be overhead. Apparently the sand is just the right diameter and consistency to create a loud noise when millions of its granules slide down the steep dune. Incredible!

Driving through Hoarusib Canyon one witnesses striking

contrasts of dark-green grasses against verdite canyon walls and near-vertical white dunes. Elephant and lion spoor (prints) are numerous. Small fish dart about in shallow ponds as lizards make their ways along the rocky walls. One then passes a fairy tale land of castles and other dynamic water-sculptured figures of sand created over eons by this stream. A rising moon places its soft loving spell over this merciless landscape. From February to April, many colorful desert flowers are in bloom.

Large game is not as evident as in Etosha National Park. Many small but just as fascinating creatures have uniquely adapted to this environment and help make this the most interesting desert in the world. Larger wildlife includes black rhino, desert elephant, lion, leopard, and baboon. Brown hyena are plentiful but not often seen. Black-backed jackals, spring-bok and gemsbok are often sighted.

Lions living along the coast have become especially adapted to living off seals, fish and birds. Lion spoor are often seen in or around camp.

The east wind brings detrite (small bits of plant matter) providing much needed compost for plants and food for lizards and beetles. The west wind brings moisture on which most life depends in this desert almost completely devoid of water.

OTHER ATTRACTIONS

The resort town of **Swakopmund**, located on the coast and surrounded by the Namib Desert, has many fine examples of German colonial architecture. The Hansa Hotel provides comfortable (Tourist Class) accommodation.

Cape Cross Seal Reserve, home of over 200,000 seals, is open daily during school and public holidays, December 16th till the end of February, and on weekends and Wednesdays. Safari companies can visit Cape Cross out of season.

THE SOUTH

NAMIB-NAUKLUFT NATIONAL PARK

The consolidation of the Namib Desert Park and the Naukluft Mountain Zebra Park and incorporation of other lands created this, the largest park in Namibia, covering 8,900 square miles of desert savannah grasslands, gypsum and quartz plains, granite mountains, a estuarine lagoon, a canyon and huge drifting apricot-colored dunes.

The Kuiseb River runs through the center of the park from east to west and acts as a natural boundary separating the northern grayish-white gravel plains from the southern deserts.

Zebra

Herds of mountain zebra, gemsbok, springbok and flocks of ostrich roam the region. The dunes are home to numerous unique creatures such as the translucent Palmato gecko, the shovel-nosed lizard and the golden mole.

The five main regions of the park are the Namib, Sandvis, Naukluft, Sesriem and Sossusvlei areas.

The **Namib** may well be the world's oldest desert. The Welwitschia-vlakte region lies on a dirt road about 22 miles north of the Swakopmund-Windhoek road and is the best area to see the pre-historic *Welwitschia mirabilis* plants. Actually classified as trees, many welwitschia are thousands of years old and are perfect examples of adaptation to an extremely hostile environment. The waterholes at Hotsas and Ganab are good locations to spot game; Ganab and Aruvlei are known for mountain zebra.

If you plan to deviate from the main road through the park, a permit is required and is obtainable weekdays only at the Nature Conservation booking offices in Swakopmund or Windhoek.

The **Sandvis** area includes Sandwich Harbour, 26 miles south of Walvis Bay and is accessible only by 4-wheel drive vehicle. Fresh water seeps into the bay from under the dunes into the salt-water lagoon resulting in a unique environment. Birdwatching is excellent September-March and at times over half a million birds are present. Only day trips are allowed to the harbour and the area is closed on Sundays. Permits are required and may be obtained from Department of Nature Conservation or from Service Stations in Walvis Bay.

The **Naukluft** region is an important watershed character-ized by dolomitic mountains over 6300 feet in height with massive picturesque rock formations and thickly foliated river beds. Large numbers of mountain zebra, along with springbok, kudu, klipspringer, rock rabbits, baboons and black eagles are frequently sighted. Also present are cheetah and leopard. The Naukluft trail is 10½ miles in length, and 6-7 hours should be allowed for the hike.

Sesriem Canyon is about 0.6 mile long and as narrow as 6 feet wide with walls about 100 feet high. When the river is high one can swim upstream where the canyon takes on a cave or tunnel-like appearance. The canyon is only a few minutes drive from Sesriem Camp (campsites only).

Sossusvlei is located in the extreme southern part of the park and has the highest sand dunes in the world, exceeding 1000 feet. As there is no camping or accommodation at Sossusvlei, plan on leaving camp at Sesriem about 5:00 am to see a spectacular sunrise on these magnificent and colorful dunes.

The base of the second-highest sand dune in the world is about a 15 minute walk from the closest point to which you can drive. The hike along the knife-edge rim to the top is strenuous, requiring 1-1½ hours of taking two-steps up and sliding one-step down. The view from the top into other valleys and of the mountains beyond is marvelous. Even up here, colorful beetles, ants, and other desert critters roam about.

My travels almost ended here when Steve Bolnick and I dune-boarded, or slid down this monster of a dune on thin, flat boards. About 900 feet down the side of the dune traveling at full speed, the front of my board caught on a large clump of grass and I flipped six times before coming to a skidding stop. My camera and compass were smashed and metal canteen crushed, but it was still a highlight of my trip — though not on my recommended list of things to do.

Driving back to camp from Sossusvlei, a gemsbok ran full speed beside our vehicle for several minutes — proving the strength and resiliency of these majestic animals.

FISH RIVER CANYON

Second in size only to the Grand Canyon, Fish River Canyon is 100 miles in length, up to 17 miles in width, and up to 1800 feet deep. The Fish River cuts its way through the canyon to the Orange River which empties into the Atlantic Ocean.

The vegetation and wildlife are very interesting. Many red aloes make the area appear like one might imagine the planet Mars. Baboons, mountain zebra, rock rabbits, ground squirrels and klipspringer are often seen, while kudu and leopard remain elusive. The river water is cold and deep enough in areas to swim.

There is a well-marked path into the canyon and basic camping facilities (no water or supplies) in the north of the park where the four-day hike begins. For those going down for the day, allow 45-60 minutes down and 1½ hours back up.

Baboon

The main hiking trail is 53 miles in length and is open May-August. The going is tough since much of the walking is on the sandy, rock-strewn floor. No facilities exist en route, so this hike is not for the tenderfoot. Water is readily available from the many pools that join to become a river during the rainy summers.

One group of 3 - 40 people is allowed per day. Permits must be obtained in advance from the Department of Nature Conservation. A medical certificate of fitness is also required.

ACCOMMODATION — CLASS C: The only accommodation is at Ai-Ais at the southern end of the canyon. Large thermally heated swimming pool, rooms with full facilities, restaurant, camping sites with cold showers, open from the second Friday in March till October 31.

RWANDA

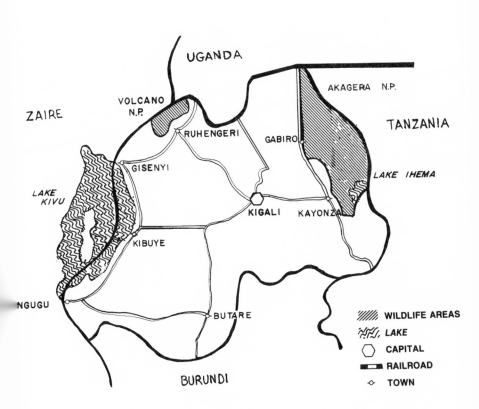

FACTS AT A GLANCE

Area:	10,169 square miles
Approximate size:	Maryland
Population:	6.4 million (1987 est.)
Capital:	Kilgali (pop. est. 150,000)
Languages:	Official: Kinyarwanda and French

Mountain gorillas are by far Rwanda's major international attraction. Travelers from all over the world venture to this remote country to experience these magnificent animals in their native environment. Watching these fascinating creatures on television is exciting enough but nothing in comparison to the thrill of visiting them first-hand.

Appropriately called "The Country of a Thousand Hills", Rwanda is predominantly grassy uplands and hills, with altitudes above sea level varying from a low of 3,960 feet to Mt. Karasimbi, the highest of a range of extinct volcanoes in the northwest, reaching almost 14,800 feet. Lake Kivu forms part of the border with Zaire and is one of the most beautiful lakes in Africa.

Also called "The Country of Perpetual Spring", Rwanda's comfortable climate is temperate and mild, with an average daytime temperature of 77° F. The main rainy season is from mid-January to mid-May, and the shorter one is from mid-October to mid-December.

Kigali is the only city, as such, in the country, and there are very few villages. Ninety-seven percent of the people live in self-contained compounds and work the adjacent land.

Christianity (mainly Catholic) is the dominant religion and many people follow traditional African beliefs. About 90% of the population is Hųtu (Bahutu), 9% Tutsi (Watusi) and 1% Twa (Batua) pygmies.

The Tutsi dominated the Hutu farmers with a feudal system analogous to that of medieval England. The system was based on cattle and was surpassed in Africa only by Ethiopia.

Because of its physical isolation and fearsome reputation, Rwanda was not affected by the slave and ivory trade from Zanzibar in the 1800's. The area peacefully became a German protectorate in 1899, and in 1916 was occupied by the Belgians.

Following World War One, Rwanda and Burundi were mandated by the League of Nations to Belgium as the territory of Ruanda-Urundi. Full independence for Rwanda and Burundi was achieved on July 1, 1962.

High population density is at the root of Rwanda's economic problems. Almost all arable land is under cultivation. Coffee is the country's major export.

Gorilla

WILDLIFE AND WILDLIFE AREAS

Although Rwanda is the most densely populated country in Africa it has set aside 15% of its land to national parks and reserves.

Rwanda has two world-class national parks — Volcano National Park and Akagera National Park. The Tourist Office (Office Rwandais du Tourisme et des Parcs Nationaux), B.P. 905, Kigali, tel: 6512, provides information on the parks.

Many tourists combine a trip to Rwanda with the parks of eastern Zaire or Kenya.

THE WEST

VOLCANO NATIONAL PARK
(PARC NATIONAL DES VOLCANS)

Volcano National Park encompasses 46 square miles; its five volcano peaks serve as a border line with Zaire and Uganda. This park is the home of the mountain gorilla which was just recently discovered in the early 1900's. The mountain gorilla is larger and has longer hair than the lowland gorilla, growing to over 6 feet in height and weighing more than 400 pounds.

Fourteen primates are found in these forests, including the red colobus and the crested mangabey. Other wildlife in the park includes forest elephants, forest hog, black-fronted duiker, yellow-backed duiker and buffalo. Over 90 species of birds have been recorded, including mountain turacos and black partridges.

Searching for gorillas in the misty mountain air of volcanos can be likened to an adventurous game of "hide and seek" in which the guides knew where they were yesterday but must find their trail again today and follow it. Finding gorillas can almost be guaranteed for those willing to hike 1-5 hours in search of them.

Each group of up to six tourists is led by a park guide. Porters may be hired and are included in most package tours to carry lunch, drinks, etc., and to assist anyone who may wish to return early.

The search often involves climbing up and down gullies and pulling yourself up steep hills by holding onto vines and bamboo. The pace is slow but you must be in good condition to keep up; the search may take you to altitudes from 7,500 to 9,800 feet. This sounds difficult, but most anyone in good physical condition without a heart problem can do it.

Mountain gorillas form themselves into groups of three to twenty. They are active only by day and sleep in nests at night. Once the gorilla group has been located, the guide communicates with them by making low grunting sounds and imitates them by picking and chewing bits of foliage. Juvenile gorillas are often found playing and tend to approach within a few feet of their human guests. In fact, occasionally our guides had to keep them from jumping into our laps.

Adult females are a little more cautious but may still approach within several feet of you. The dominant male is called a silverback because of the silvery-grey hair on his back.

Gorilla-viewing "etiquette" is important. Do not make eye contact with a silverback. If the silverback begins to act aggressively, look down immediately and take a submissive posture by squatting or sitting down or he may take your staring as an act of aggression and charge. The key is to follow the directions of your well-trained guide. Gorillas are herbivores (vegetarians) and will not attack a man unless provoked.

After spending from 30-60 minutes visiting with these magnificent animals visitors descend to a more open area for a picnic lunch.

The groups visited by tourists have been numbered or named by researchers studying them. Two groups (11 and 13) make Rwanda their permanent home. Visitors to Group 11 meet at the Visoke departure point. Muside has two departure points for visitors to Group 13, Karandagi or Kanuma, so be sure to learn which is your departure point at park headquarters.

Group 9 divides its time between Rwanda and Zaire, and therefore permits are sold only at the park headquarters at Kiningi up to one day in advance.

Group Susa can be visited by a maximum of two people on an overnight stay. A three-hour hike brings you to the tin shelter where you spend the night. Gorillas are visited the following morning with a return to Kinigi in the afternoon. Bring your own sleeping bag and food.

Groups 11 & 13 must be booked in advance at the tourist office in Kigali, while Group 9 can only be booked at Volcano

National Park Headquarters near Kinigi. Permits for group Susa may be purchased in Kinigi or Kigali. Children under eight years of age are not allowed to visit group 11 and no children under 15 are allowed to visit group 13.

Visitors must check in at park headquarters near Kinigi village, about a 45-minute drive from Ruhengeri, between 7:00 — 8:00 am. Be sure to have your voucher before making the 30-40 minute (10 mile) drive to departure points where the searches begin. Visitors must meet their guides at designated departure points no later than 9:00 am.

Hiking in itself is an adventure. Trails lead to the craters or peaks of the park's five volcanos, upwards through the unique high-vegetation zones of bamboo, hagenia-hypericum forests, giant lobelia and senecio, and finally to alpine meadows. Many travelers spend a day or two searching for gorillas interspaced with hikes to one or more of the volcanos.

Karasimbi (14,786 ft.) is Rwanda's highest and occasionally snow-capped mountain and the most arduous ascent, requiring two days from the Visoke departure point. Visoke (12,175 ft.) has a beautiful crater lake and requires four hours of hiking up a steep trail to reach the summit from the Visoke departure point. The walk around the crater rim is highly recommended.

Ngezi Lake (9,843 ft.) is a small, shallow crater lake, the easiest hike in the park, taking only 3-4 hours roundtrip from the Visoke departure point. Sabinyo (11,922 ft.) can be climbed in 5-6 hours starting at the park headquarters near Kinigi. The final section is along a narrow rocky ridge with steep drops on both sides.

Gahinga (11,398 ft.) and Muhabura (13,540 ft.) are both reached from the departure point at Gasiza. The trail rises to a cabin in poor condition on the saddle between the two mountains. Gahinga's summit can be reached in four hours, while two days are recommended to reach the summit of Muhabura.

ACCOMMODATION — DELUXE: see Gisenyi.

CLASS C: • Hotel Muhabura is the best hotel in Ruhengeri and has the most convenient access to Volcano National Park (45-minute drive). Bathrooms en-suite, popular bar and dining room. Chauffeured mini-bus available for hire to the park.

CAMPING: At Park Headquarters near Kinigi and other sites.

GISENYI

Picturesque resort on beautiful Lake Kivu with sandy white beaches believed to have little or no bilharzia. Crocodiles are absent from the lake due to volcanic action eons ago which wiped them out, making swimming safer.

ACCOMMODATION — DELUXE: • Hotel Izuba Meridien, excellent hotel serving superb cuisine, located 1¾ hour drive from Volcano National Park.

TOURIST CLASS • Hotel Palm Beach.

OTHER REGIONS

KIGALI

The capital of Rwanda, Kigali is the commercial center of the country and has little of interest for the tourist. There are very good restaurants in the deluxe hotels.

ACCOMMODATION — DELUXE: • Hotel des Diplomats. • Hotel des Milles Collines. • Umubano Meridien. All three hotels are excellent.

TOURIST CLASS: • Hotel Kiyovu.

AKAGERA NATIONAL PARK
(LE PARC NATIONAL DE L'AKAGERA)

Akagera National Park is located in northeastern Rwanda along the Akagera River (a Nile affluent) bordering Tanzania. Over 500,000 animals of great variety inhabit the park, including the largest species of buffalo in Africa, along with zebra, hippo, lion, leopard, impala, waterbuck, eland, tapir, crocodile, sable, oribi, roan, and jackals. This is the best place in Africa to see sitatunga, which are often spotted from towers overlooking the swamps. Rhino, elephant and leopard are seen rarely, and there are no giraffe. Bird-life is excellent with 525 species of birds recorded — a record for any park or region of this size.

Akagera National Park covers 980 square miles (10% of the country's area), and can be divided into three regions.

The northern part of the park is predominantly low treeless hills interspaced with both dry and marshy valleys. Buffalo, zebra, waterbuck, topi, and many other species of herbivore

Sitatunga

Buffalo

prefer this region. Herds of animals numbering in the thousands can be seen, especially in the dry season. Interestingly enough, buffalo, zebra and topi are much larger than those found in East Africa. Some buffalo males weigh in excess of 2200 pounds with shoulder heights of 6 feet and horn widths of 3.5 feet.

The second region is the most unique and is possibly the best preserved and most diverse swamp in terms of both flora and fauna in East and East-Central Africa. It is composed of three large swamps separated by lakes along the eastern border of the park. Papyrus dominates the swamps. Large numbers of waterfowl, including herons, ducks, storks, waders and plovers can be seen in areas with floating ferns, swamp grasses and water lilies.

At the fishing station (Pêcherie) on Lake Ihema, the largest of the lakes, boats can be rented or you may join irregularly scheduled group departures to the islands and far shores of the lake. Fresh fish is fried there almost every afternoon and is some of the best I've ever eaten. A few tame elephants may be seen for a small fee at Lulama. Feed them some sugarcane and get some great photos! Plage aux Hippos (Hippo Beach) on Mihindi Lake has picnic facilities and is a great spot for watching hippos, crocodiles and waterfowl.

Hippopotamus

The third region covers the central and southern areas lying west of the swamps and is characterized by more trees and thicker vegetation than the northern region.

Relatively good all-weather tracks run for 280 miles through the park, marked with numbered crossroads. Stay in your vehicle, except at marked picnic spots, camping or hotel grounds. Guides are available for hire at the gates.

The best time to visit the park is during the dry season, July to September, while February, June and October are also good. ACCOMMODATION — CLASS A: • Akagera Hotel, modern hotel overlooking Lake Ihema, swimming pool, bar, restaurant.

CLASS B: • Gabiro Hotel, located at Byumba at the edge of the park, rustic atmosphere.

CAMPING: Several sites are within the park. Permits may have to be obtained in advance from the Rwanda Tourist Office in Kigali.

SOUTH AFRICA

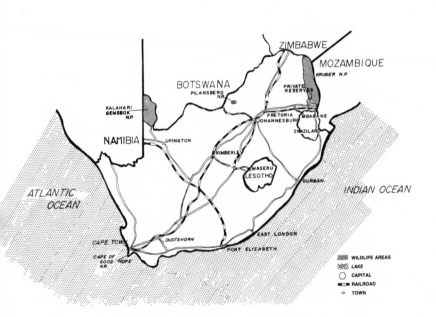

FACTS AT A GLANCE

Area:	437,000 square miles
Approximate size:	More than 3 times the size of Texas
Population:	31 million (1987 est.)
Capital:	Pretoria (pop. est. 547,280)
Languages:	Official: English and Afrikaans

South Africa is a large country rich in natural beauty and wildlife whose actual size has been made much larger by the news. Actually, it covers less than 3.8% of the continent.

Seventy percent of the total population belongs to four ethnic groups — Zulu (the largest), Xhosa, Tswana and Bapedi. Fifteen percent of the population is white of which 60% are Afrikaners. English and Afrikaans are spoken throughout the country.

In 1488 the Portuguese navigator Bartholomew Dias discovered the Cape of Good Hope. The first Dutch settlers arrived in 1652 and the first British settlers in 1820. In order to escape British rule, Boer (meaning farmer) Voortrekkers (meaning forward marchers) moved to the north and east and established the independent republics of the Transvaal and Orange Free State.

Two very big economic breakthroughs were the discovery of diamonds in 1869, and even more importantly, the discovery of gold in the Transvaal shortly thereafter. Conflict between the British and the Boers resulted in the Anglo-Boer War from 1899 until British victory in 1902.

In 1910 the Union of South Africa was formed and remained a member of the British Commonwealth until May 31, 1961 when The Republic of South Africa was formed outside the British Commonwealth.

WILDLIFE AND WILDLIFE AREAS

The parks, reserves and sanctuaries in South Africa are very well organized and maintained, and in many ways similar to those in North America. Accommodation in the national parks is clean, comfortable, and inexpensive. Campers share ablution blocks with running hot & cold water, and many sites have laundromats. The facilities and infrastructure make this country an excellent choice for self-drive safaris.

Generally speaking, the major roads in the parks are tarred with the minor ones constructed of good quality gravel, allowing for comfortable riding. Tourists must stay in their vehicles except where specifically permitted, and cannot leave the roads in search of game. Open vehicles are not allowed in the parks, and roof hatches on vehicles must remain closed. Reservations for all national parks can be made by contacting The Chief Director, National Parks Board, P.O. Box 787, Pretoria 0001; tel: (012) 44-1191; telex: 32-1324 SA.

THE TRANSVAAL

JOHANNESBURG

Johannesburg began as a mining town when the largest deposits of gold in the world were discovered in the Witwatersrand in 1886. One-third of the gold mined in the world since the Middle Ages has come from the Witwatersrand field. This "City of Gold" is now the country's largest commercial center and city (pop. two million), and main gateway for visitors from overseas. Attractions include the Africana Museum (excellent), the Gold Mine Museum, and Gold Reef City, a reconstruction of Johannesburg at the turn of the century.

ACCOMMODATION — DELUXE: • Johannesburg Sun, newly constructed, the largest hotel in Africa. • Landdrost, centrally located, three restaurants, three bars, shops, nightclub. • Sandton Sun, 10 miles from Johannesburg in one of the country's finest shopping malls. Elegant, sophisticated, spacious rooms and suites, swimming pool, five restaurants including the exquisite "Chapters." • Carlton Hotel, in a large mall. • Gold Reef City Hotel, beautifully decorated with turn-of-the-century furniture.

FIRST CLASS: Rand International, well located in the center of town, large rooms and suites, excellent dining. • Hotel Braamfontein, on the edge of downtown Johannesburg within walking distance of air and train terminals. All rooms are suites.

TOURIST CLASS • Diplomat Hotel, centrally located, rooms with bath, restaurant, bar.

KRUGER AND THE PRIVATE RESERVES

The most popular area of the country for wildlife safaris is Kruger National Park and the private reserves that lie along its western border. The best game viewing for this region is June-September (the very best is July-August) during the sunny, dry winter season when the grass has been grazed down and the deciduous plants have lost their leaves. This is also the best time to hike the wilderness trails in Kruger and take foot safaris in the private reserves. Calving season is in early spring (September-October) for most game species.

Winter days are usually warm with an average maximum of 73° F and clear skies. Late afternoons are cool, while temperatures at night and early morning sometimes drop below freezing. From October to February there are light rains, with December, January and February receiving the heaviest downpours with temperatures sometimes rising to 104° F. March and April are cooler and the rains begin to diminish.

The best time to look for the over 450 bird species in this region is from October to March — just the opposite of the best game viewing periods. However, birdwatching is good year-round since less than half the bird population is composed of seasonal migrants.

To get to the area, fly from Johannesburg to Skukuza or Phalaborwa with Comair. Guests of Sabi Sabi, Mala Mala and Londolozi are met at Skukuza. Avis rentals are available. The drive from Johannesburg to Kruger is on tarred roads and takes 5-6 hours.

Open Land Rover with Elephant

KRUGER NATIONAL PARK

Kruger is the largest South African park and has more species of wildlife than any other game sanctuary in Africa: 130 species of mammal, 114 species of reptile, 48 species of fish, 33 species of amphibians, and 468 species of birds.

The park is home to large population of elephant, buffalo, Burchell's zebra, greater kudu, giraffe, impala, white rhino, black rhino, hippopotamus, lion, leopard, cheetah, wild or cape hunting dog and spotted hyena, among others.

Kruger's 7,700 square miles make it nearly the size of the state of Massachusetts. The park is 55 miles wide at its widest point and 220 miles long. It is totally fenced, cutting off the annual winter migration routes of antelope, zebra and various other species in search of water and better grazing. Several hundred windmills and artificial waterholes have been constructed to provide water desperately needed in the dry season.

The park can be divided into three major regions — northern, central/southeastern, and southwestern. Altitude varies from 650 feet in the east to 2,950 feet at Pretoriuskop in the southwest.

The northern region from the Letaba River to the Limpopo River is the driest. Mopane trees dominate the landscape, with the unique Baobab (upside-down) trees becoming increasingly numerous towards Pafuri and the Limpopo River. From Letaba to Punda Maria is the best region for spotting elephant, tsessebe, sable and roan antelope. Elephant prefer this area since it is less developed than the other regions, making it easier to congregate away from roads and traffic, and the prevalence of mopane trees — their preferred source of food.

The central/southeastern region is situated south of Letaba to Orpen Gate and includes the eastern part of the park from Satara southward covering Nwanedzi, Lower Sable and Crocodile Bridge. Grassy plains and scattered knobthorn, leadwood, and marula trees dominate the landscape. Lion inhabit most areas of the park but are most prevalent in this region where there is also an abundance of zebra and wildebeest — their favorite prey. Cheetah and black-backed jackal are best spotted on the plains. Wild or cape hunting dogs are mainly scattered throughout flatter areas, with possibly a better chance of finding them in the Letaba-Malopene River area and northwest of Malelane.

The southwestern part of the park, including a wide strip along the western boundary from Skukuza to Orpen Gate, is more densely forested with thorny thickets, knobthorn, marula and red bush-willow. This is the most difficult region in which to spot game — especially during the rainy season. Many of the park's 600 white rhino prefer this area.

Black rhino are scattered throughout the southern and central areas, often feeding on low-lying acacia trees. Leopards are rarely seen. Buffalo roam throughout the park, while hippo prefer to inhabit the deeper parts of Kruger's many rivers by day.

Four different two-day/three-night wilderness trails (walking safaris) are conducted twice weekly by experienced game rangers: Olifants, Nyalaland, Wolhuter and Bushman Trails. These walks take an easy pace in order to explore the natural beauty of the bush and to experience spotting game on foot. A maximum of eight participants between 12 and 60 years of age are allowed per safari. Trails begin at their respective meeting places at 3:00 p.m. on Mondays or Fridays and end after breakfast on the third day.

The Automobile Association of South Africa patrols the park, assisting its membership. During school holidays and long weekends the number of day visitors is limited, so be sure to reserve in advance.

ACCOMMODATION — There are 16 rest camps offering a wide range of comfortable accommodation including cottages with private bath (Class C), thatched huts with or without private facilities (Class D), and camping sites. The larger rest camps have licensed restaurants.

THE PRIVATE RESERVES

Along the western border of Kruger lie a number of privately owned wildlife reserves. These reserves are associations of ranchers who have fenced around each reserve but have not fenced their individual properties, allowing game to freely roam within each reserve. The private reserves, in general, have exceptionally high standards of accommodation, food and service.

A very important advantage private reserves have over the national parks is that private reserves use open vehicles which give not only a better view but also a much better feel of the bush. At most reserves, a game tracker sits on the hood or the back of each vehicle. Drivers are in radio contact with each other, greatly increasing the chances of finding those species that guests want to see most.

Vehicles may leave the road to pursue game through the bush. Night drives, which are not allowed in Kruger, provide an opportunity to spot game rarely seen during the day. Full room and board and two game drives per day are usually included in the package price.

ACCOMMODATION — Sabi-Sand Private Game Reserve is situated to the north and northwest of Skukuza, and includes Sabi Sabi, Mala Mala, Londolozi and Inyati.

CLASS A: • Sabi Sabi, deluxe accommodation at Bush Lodge and River Lodge, both with air conditioning, swimming pools, excellent food. Atmosphere is casual, the experienced staff warm and friendly. • Mala Mala Game Reserve has three facilities: Mala Mala (Class A), Kirkman's Kamp (Class B) and Harry's (Class C).

CLASS B: • Inyati Game Lodge, thatched chalets with full facilities. • Tanda Tula, on the Timbavati Game Reserve renowned for its population of rare white lions.

CLASS C: • Londolozi Game Reserve, on the banks of the Sabi River, rustic accommodation cooled by ceiling fans.

CAPE PROVINCE

CAPE TOWN

Sir Francis Drake once said of the Cape Town area: "The fairest cape we saw in the whole circumference of the globe." Today Cape Town is thought to be by many well-traveled people one of the most beautiful settings in the world.

The cable ride (or 3 hour hike) up **Table Mountain** is a must, with breathtaking views. Bring warm clothing since it is usually much cooler and windier on top. An afternoon champagne cruise past islands with hundreds of seals, rocky cliffs and sandy beaches allows a delightful new perspective to the area.

The Cape reminds me of the California coast — stark, natural beauty and a laid-back atmosphere. The drive through the **Cape of Good Hope Nature Reserve** to Cape Point where the Atlantic meets the Indian Ocean is one of the finest drives on the continent.

Seapoint is bustling with nightlife, with many distinctive restaurants, bistros and bars. **Kirstenbosch National Botanical Gardens**, one of the finest gardens in the world, has 9,000 of the 21,000 flowering plants of Southern Africa.

February-March is the best time to visit the Cape when there is very little wind; October-January is warm and windy; May-August rainy.

Stellenbosch is the center of the wine industry, and a half to a full day should be taken to visit a few wineries such as Blaauklippen.

Some of the finer restaurants include Belvedere House, La Vita, and The Wooden Bridge, across Table Bay, which is exceptionally nice in summer; guests watch the sun set behind Table Mountain.

ACCOMMODATION — DELUXE: • Cape Sun, modern hotel with a great view of the harbor. • Heerengracht, sophisticated hotel, swimming pool, in the center of the business district. • Mount Nelson, old-world British hotel set on seven landscaped acres.

KALAHARI GEMSBOK NATIONAL PARK

Located in the northwest corner of South Africa and sharing borders with Botswana and Namibia, this 3,700 square mile park is predominately semi-desert and part desert. Scattered thorn trees and grasses lie between red Kalahari sand dunes. Bushmen inhabited the area as much as 25,000 years ago.

The park features large herds of blue wildebeest, eland, springbok, and the stately gemsbok with their long, straight spear-like horns. Also present are red hartebeest, duiker, steenbok, Kalahari lion, cheetah, brown hyena and wild dog.

Summer temperatures can exceed 104° F. Winter days are pleasant but temperatures can drop below freezing at night. Wells provide water for the animals which have adapted to desert conditions by eating plants with high water content such as wild cucumber and tsamma melon.

There are three rest camps with self-contained cottages with kitchens (Class D), huts with and without bathrooms, camping sites, stores, petrol and diesel. There is a swimming pool at Twee Rivieren, an information center about the plant and animal life at Nossob, and landing strips for small aircraft at both camps. Cars may be hired from the Parks Board. Visits to the park by vehicle can also be arranged by the town Council of Upington.

OTHER ATTRACTIONS

One of the prettiest drives on the continent, the Garden Route runs from Jeffrey's Bay to Swellendam between Port

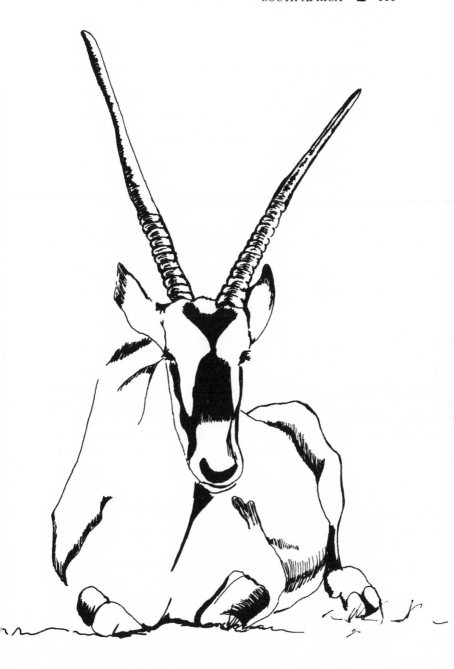

Gemsbok

Ostrich

Elizabeth and Capetown. Rain falls throughout the year keeping the route luxuriously green.

Oudtshoorn is where you go to ride an ostrich — or at least watch them race and tour a farm. I have some great pictures of me flying through the air after the bird apparently tired of having me on its back.

Kimberley is the "diamond city" where one of the biggest strikes occurred in 1868. Visit the open air museum and the "Big Hole" where over three tons of diamonds were removed from the largest man-dug hole in the world.

Cheetah

The **Pilansberg Nature Reserve**, located in Bophuthatswana, is a small reserve covering about 200 square miles. Wildlife includes black and white rhino, elephant, eland, sable, leopard, and cheetah. Kwa Maritane provides comfortable cabana accommodation (Class A) with swimming pool.

Sun City is a premier entertainment vacation complex located nearby with Vegas-style floor shows, casino, golf, tennis, and water sports. The Cascades (Deluxe) is a luxurious hotel spectacularly designed and landscaped with lush gardens, waterfalls, and swimming pool, and cuisine fit for a king. Sun City Hotel and Cabanas (First Class) have full facilities in a spacious setting.

TANZANIA

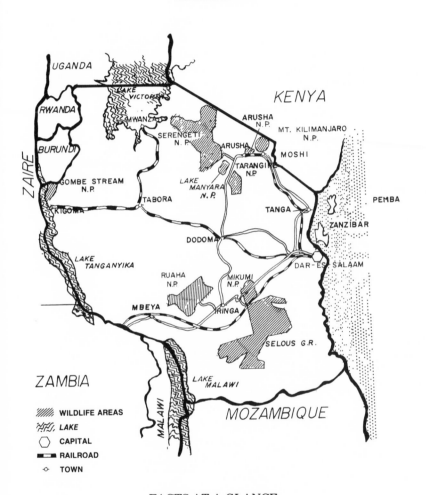

FACTS AT A GLANCE

Area:	363,708 square miles
Approximate size:	Texas + Oklahoma
Population:	22 million (1987 est.)
Capital:	Dar es Salaam (pop. est. 750,000)
Official Language:	Official: Kiswahili; English widely spoken

Between Africa's highest mountain (Kilimanjaro) and Africa's largest lake (Victoria) lies one of the best game viewing areas on the continent. This region also includes the world's largest intact volcanic crater (Ngorongoro) and the most famous wildlife park (the Serengeti). To the south lies the world's largest reserve — the Selous.

Volcanic highlands dominate the north giving way southward to a plateau, then semi-desert in the center of the country and highlands in the south. The coastal lowlands are hot and humid with lush vegetation. One branch of the Great Rift Valley passes through Lakes Manyara and Natron in northern Tanzania to Lake Nyasa (Lake Malawi) in the south while the other passes through Lakes Rukwa and Tanganyika in the west.

Heavy rains occur from mid-February to mid-May, and lighter rains October-November. Altitude has a great effect on temperature. At Arusha (4,600 ft.) and the Ngorongoro Crater (7,500 ft.) nights and early mornings are especially cool. Tanzania's highest temperatures occur in November and lowest in July.

Evidence suggests East Africa as the cradle of mankind. The earliest known humanoid footprints, estimated to be 3.5 million years old, were discovered at Laetoli by Dr. Mary Leakey in 1979, who in 1957 also found the estimated 1.75 million year-old skull *Zinjanthropus boisei* at Olduvai Gorge.

By the 13th century Arabs, Persians, Egyptians, Indians and Chinese were involved in heavy trading on the coast. Slave trade began in the mid 1700's and was abolished in 1873.

British Explorers Richard Burton and John Speke crossed Tanzania in 1857 to Lake Tanganyika. Speke later discovered Lake Victoria which he felt was the source of the Nile.

The German East Africa Company gained control of the mainland (then called German East Africa) in 1885, and the German government took over from 1891 until World War One when it was mandated to Britain by the League of Nations. Tanganyika gained its independence from Britain in 1961 and Zanzibar in 1963. Zanzibar, once the center of the East African slave trade, was ruled by sultans until its union with Tanganyika in 1964 forming the United Republic of Tanzania.

There are 120 tribes in Tanzania. Bantu dialects are spoken by 95% of the population, with Kiswahili the most universal and national language. Over 90% of the people are peasant farmers. The export of coffee, cotton, sisal, tea, cloves and cashews bring 70% of the country's foreign exchange.

WILDLIFE AND WILDLIFE AREAS

Reserves cover over 95,000 square miles of area — probably more than any other country on earth. Not as much game is seen in Tanzania outside the reserves as in Kenya, perhaps because hunting is still allowed in Tanzania.

The peak tourist seasons are from July through October and December-March; August is the busiest month. Heavy rains fall in April and May, hampering travel and game viewing. The calving season for wildebeest is from mid-January to mid-March. For information and reservations contact the Tanzania National Parks, P.O. Box 3134, Arusha.

THE NORTH

This region from Mt. Kilimanjaro in the east to Serengeti National Park in the west is the area most visited by tourists and contains the country's most famous parks.

The Northern Circuit traditionally includes Lake Manyara National Park, Ngorongoro Conservation Area, Olduvai Gorge, and Serengeti National Park.

From Arusha drive 45 miles west to Makuyuni, then either continue on the main road another 20 miles to Tarangire National Park, or turn right (northwest) to Lake Manyara National Park. After passing Lake Manyara the road climbs the Rift Valley escarpment and the slopes of the Ngorongoro Crater. The road descends the western side of the mountain to the Olduvai Gorge and Serengeti National Park.

ARUSHA

This town is the center of tourism for northern Tanzania and is situated on the foothills of rugged Mt. Meru. Named after the Arusha tribe, it is located on the Great North Road mid-way between Cairo and Capetown.
ACCOMMODATION — • CLASS C: Mt. Meru Hotel, located at the foot of Mt. Meru, swimming pool.
CLASS D: • New Arusha Hotel, beautiful gardens, swimming pool.

LAKE MANYARA NATIONAL PARK

Once one of the most popular hunting areas of Tanzania, this 123 square mile park has the Great Rift Valley escarpment for a dramatic backdrop. Two-thirds of the park is covered by alkaline Lake Manyara.

Five different vegetation zones are found in the park. The first zone reached from the park entrance is groundwater forest fed by water seeping from the Great Rift Wall, with wild fig, sausage, tamarind and mahogany trees. Elephant prefer these dense forests as well as marshy glades. The other zones include the marshlands along the edge of the lake, scrub on Rift Valley Wall, open areas with scattered acacia, and open grasslands.

Manyara, like Ishasha in the Ruwenzori National Park in Uganda, is infamous for its tree-climbing lions found lazing on branches of acacia trees. It is believed that lions climb trees in Manyara to avoid tsetse flies and the dense undergrowth while remaining in the cool shade, while lions of the Ruwenzori National Park in Uganda climb trees to gain a hunting advantage. Finding lion in the trees is not guaranteed so don't set your heart on it — look at it as an unexpected bonus.

At the hippo pool we saw over 20 gregarious hippos lying all over each other in a pile on the bank. Something finally spooked them and a mad rush ensued as they joined other hippos in the pool.

Manyara features large concentrations of elephant and buffalo. Black rhino and leopard are rare. Game viewing is good year-round since many of the animals are permanent residents, with the best time being during the dry seasons. Other wildlife includes waterbuck, giraffe, zebra, impala, baboons and sykes monkeys. Over 380 species of birds, including over 30 birds of prey, have been recorded.

Roads are good year-round and 4-wheel drive is not needed, although in the rainy season some side tracks may be temporarily closed. Guides are available for a small fee.

ACCOMMODATION — CLASS C: • Lake Manyara Hotel, magnificent setting on the Rift Valley Escarpment overlooking the park and the Rift Valley 1,000 feet below. Swimming pool, bar, restaurant, and airstrip.

CAMPING: Sites are located near the park entrance.

NGORONGORO CRATER CONSERVATION AREA

Ngorongoro is the largest intact crater in the world. Its vastness and beauty is truly overwhelming and is believed by some to have been the proverbial Garden of Eden. Ngorongoro contains possibly the largest permanent concentration of wildlife in Africa. Many scientists believe that before this volcano erupted it was larger than Mt. Kilimanjaro.

The crater itself is but a small portion of the 2,500 square mile Ngorongoro Conservation Area. The crater is about 12 miles wide and its rim rises 1,200 - 1,600 feet off its expansive 102 square mile floor. From the crater rim elephant appear as small dark specks on the grasslands. A shallow soda lake near its center attracts thousands of flamingos and other birdlife. The Masai are allowed to bring in their cattle by day for grazing but must leave the crater at night.

The steep decent into the crater along a narrow rough winding road takes 30-45 minutes. A guide is no longer required and any 4-wheel drive vehicles are allowed.

Large concentrations of wildlife make Ngorongoro their permanent home, so game viewing is good year-round. We saw black rhino, including one mother with her baby, lion, elephant, buffalo, zebra, wildebeest, flamingos, baboons, monkeys, kori bustards and a host of other species. Elephant are often found in the wooded areas and on the slopes of the crater. Cheetah are also present, but there are no giraffe.

At the picnic site vervets are very aggressive in getting at your food. Kites (a species of bird) made many swooping attempts at our lunches. Overnight camping is allowed in the crater for those who bring all their equipment. A guide must accompany the group for a small fee.

One important thing to remember: game is not confined to the crater; many animals leave at night to forage elsewhere, including near the hotels and lodges. This I learned the hard way one night on my first visit to Ngorongoro. Just outside of the Ngorongoro Wildlife Lodge, blindly I walked within 20 feet of three large buffalo. One buffalo appeared as if it was going to charge, then fortunately they ran off. Welcome to Africa!, I thought.

About 30 miles west of Ngorongoro Crater a few miles off the road to the Serengeti is the **Olduvai Gorge**. Site of many archeological discoveries including the estimated 1¾ million year-old *Zinjanthropus boisei* fossil, now housed in the National Museum in Dan es Salaam.

ACCOMMODATION — CLASS C: • Ngorongoro Wildlife Lodge, a beautiful hotel, spectacular views of the crater, large lounge and dining area, veranda with telescopes, good service • Ngorongoro Crater Lodge, bandas with bathrooms, older than the Wildlife Lodge • Gibb's Farm, 15 miles from the crater, very good food.

CAMPING: On the Ngorongoro Crater floor and other sites within the conservation area.

SERENGETI NATIONAL PARK

This is Tanzania's most famous park and has the largest concentration of migratory game animals in the world. It is also famous for its huge lion population and is probably the best place on the continent to see them. The park has received great notoriety through Professor Bernard Grzimek's book *Serengeti Shall Not Die.*

The park's 5,600 square miles make it larger than the state of Connecticut. It borders on the north with Kenya's Masai Mara National Reserve, on the southeast with the Ngorongoro Conservation Area, and on the west the "corridor" comes within a few miles of Lake Victoria. Altitude varies from 3,000 -6,000 feet.

Most of the Serengeti is vast open plain broken by rocky outcrops (koppies). There are also acacia savannah, savannah

Lion

woodland, riverine forests, some swamps and small lakes. Thick scrub and forests line the Mara River in the north, where leopards are sometimes spotted sleeping in the trees. Savannah dominates the central region, with open plains in the south and woodland plains and hills in the western corridor. The Masai still herd their cattle in the park.

Topi

Wildebeest

In the Serengeti over 350 species of birds and 35 species of plains animals can be found. The park may contain as many as 1.5 million wildebeest, 750,000 gazelle and half-million zebra. The best time to visit is December-May when the game is most highly concentrated.

It is impossible to predict the exact time of the famous migration. From December-May wildebeest, zebra, eland and Thomson's gazelle usually concentrate in the southeastern region of the park near Lake Ndutu in search of short grass which they prefer over the longer dry-stemmed variety. May is in fact a good time to visit this region of the Serengeti as long as you are traveling in a 4-wheel drive vehicle.

During the long rainy season (April-May) nomadic lions and hyena move to the eastern part of the Serengeti. The migration, mainly of wildebeest and zebra, begins in May or June.

Wildebeest move about 6 - 10 abreast in columns several miles long towards the western corridor. Zebra do not move in columns but in family units.

By June or July the migration has usually progressed west of Seronera. The migration then splits into three separate migrations, one west through the corridor towards permanent water and Lake Victoria and then northeast, one due north reaching Masai Mara of Kenya around mid-July, and the third northwards between the other two to a region west of Lobo Lodge where the group disperses. Driving off the roads is not permitted in the park and at present there are no roads in region where the third group disperses, although this may soon change.

July-September the Serengeti's highest concentration of wildlife is in the extreme north. The first and second groups meet and begin returning to the Serengeti National Park around the end of September/early October, and reach the southern Serengeti by December.

Seronera Lodge, park headquarters and the park village are located together in the center of the park. Game plentiful in the area includes hyenas, cheetah, jackals, topi, giraffe, and Thomson's gazelle. Large numbers of giraffe are permanent residents in the north near Lobo Lodge.

ACCOMMODATION — CLASS C: • Ndutu Tented Camp, located near the border of the Ngorongoro Conservation Area.

CLASS D: • Seronera Wildlife Lodge, centrally located, often experiences water problems. • Lobo Wildlife Lodge, in the north 50 miles from the Kenyan border, uniquely designed around huge boulders and has a swimming pool carved out of solid rock.

Grant's Gazelle

CAMPING: Several campsites available.

TARANGIRE NATIONAL PARK

Large numbers of baobab trees dotting the landscape give the park a prehistoric look the likes of which I have never seen. This park has a different feel to it than any other northern park — and an eerie feeling at that, making it one of my favorites.

Fewer tourists visit this park than Manyara, Ngorongoro and Serengeti, allowing a better opportunity to experience it as the early explorers did — alone.

We spotted eland, giraffe, buffalo, a few lion, oryx, elephant, impala, Grant's gazelles, zebra, hartebeest, warthogs, baboons, ostrich, and the carcass of an elephant that we were told has been shot outside the park and wandered in to die. We met one group that kept their fires burning all night to keep three lions they had heard near the camp at bay!

Elephants have destroyed many baobab trees and a baobab tree with a huge hole through the center of its trunk can be seen near the lodge.

Game viewing is best in this 1,000 square mile park during the dry season from July-September, which happens to be the worst months for viewing game in the Serengeti. Consequently visitors to Tanzania during those months might consider substituting Tarangire for the Serengeti should there not be time for both, or at least try to add Tarangire to the itinerary. Tarangire can be visited in a day from Lake Manyara National Park. Birdwatching is best December-May.

ACCOMMODATION — CLASS C: • Tarangire Safari Lodge, new lodge set on a hill with two swimming pools (one for children), restaurant, tents and bandas.

CAMPING: Sites within the park. No Facilities.

MOUNT KILIMANJARO NATIONAL PARK

Known to many through Ernest Hemingway's book *The Snows of Kilimanjaro*, this is the highest mountain in the world not part of a range and is definitely one of the world's most impressive mountains. Kilimanjaro means "shining mountain" and rises from an altitude of about 3,000 feet on the dry plains to 19,340 feet. On clear days the mountain can be seen from over 200 miles away.

The mountain consists of three major volcanic centers: Kibo (19,340 ft.), Shira (13,650 ft.) to the west and Mawenzi (16,893 ft.) to the east. The park covers 292 square miles of the mountain above the upper tree limit of the Kilimanjaro Forest Reserve. Hikers pass through zones of forest, alpine, and semi-desert to its snow-capped peak situated only three degrees south of the equator. It was once thought to be an extinct volcano but due to recent rumblings it is now classified as dormant.

Climbing Mt. Kilimanjaro was definitely a highlight of my travels. For the struggle to reach its highest peak I was handsomely rewarded with a feeling of accomplishment with many exciting memories of the climb.

Kilimanjaro is in fact the easiest mountain in the world to ascend to such heights, but it is still a struggle for even fit adventurers. On the other hand, it can and is climbed by people from all walks of life who are in good condition and have a strong will. Mind you, reaching the top is by no means necessary; the flora, fauna and magnificent views seen en route are fabulous.

The most unique animal in this park is the Abbot's duiker which is found in only a few mountain forests in northern Tanzania. Other wildlife includes elephant, black rhino, buffalo, eland, leopard, hyrax, and black and white colobus monkeys; very little large game is seen.

The best time to climb is during January, February, September and October during the dryer seasons when the skies are fairly clear. December, March, July, August are good, while April, May and November should be avoided because of heavy rains and overcast skies. I, of course, happened to be in Tanzania in April and climbed anyway.

Climbing Kibo via many routes including the "tourist route" requires no mountaineering skills. A guide for each climbing party is required, while porters are optional though highly recommended.

The Marangu (tourist) Route may be completed in five days but it's best to take six days to allow more time to acclimatize to the altitude. Your guide will prepare all your meals for you. The huts are dormitory-style with common areas for cooking and eating. Several American tour operators take other routes up and return via the Marangu Route, offering additional variety to the climb.

I met an American doctor working in Moshi who actually climbed the mountain by himself (without guide or porters) in less than 24 hours. His theory was that if you climb quickly, altitude sickness does not have time to set in. I suggest, though, that you take your time.

Mountaineers wishing to ascend by more difficult routes may wish to contact the Mountain Club of Kenya (P.O. Box, Nairobi, Kenya) for advice. Mawenzi peak should only be attempted by well-equipped, experienced mountaineers. Permission must be obtained from the park warden before climbing any other route besides Marangu.

Park headquarters are located in Marangu (Kilimanjaro National Park, P.O. Box 96, Marangu; tel: Marangu 50), 30 miles from Moshi. All-inclusive climbs are arranged for parties by the Kibo Hotel, the Marangu Hotel, the Moshi YMCA.
ACCOMMODATION — CLASS C: • Kibo Hotel. Marangu Hotel. Good food.

OTHER ATTRACTIONS

Arusha National Park is predominately inhabited by forest animals while in the other northern parks savannah animals the most prevalent. This is the best place in northern Tanzania to spot black and white colobus monkeys and bushbuck, and to photograph larger species with Mt. Kilimanjaro in the background. Early mornings are best for this since Mt. Kilimanjaro is less likely to be covered with clouds. Wildlife is more difficult to spot here than in the other northern parks; do not expect to see large herds of game. The best time to visit is July to March.

This 45 square mile park is actually the merger of three regions: Meru Crater National Park, the Momella Lakes, and Ngurdoto Crater National Park. The wide range of habitats from highland rain forest to acacia woodlands and crater lakes host a variety of wildlife. There are no lions which makes walking much safer.

The Momella Game Lodge has rondavels (Class D) outside the gate. Camping sites are available.

THE SOUTH AND WEST

SELOUS GAME RESERVE

This little-known reserve happens to be the largest game reserve in the world. Over 21,000 square miles in area, the Selous is more than half the size of the state of Ohio and 3¾ times larger than Serengeti National Park. Unexploited and largely unexplored, no human habitation is allowed in this virgin bush except for limited tourist facilities.

The Selous is a stronghold for over 50,000 elephant (recently down from 100,000 due to rampant poaching), 150,000 buffalo, and large populations of black rhino, lion, leopard, sable antelope, Lichtenstein's hartebeest, greater

Black Rhino

kudu, hippo, crocodiles, and numerous other species. Over one million large animals live within its borders. Game is plentiful but more patience is required to spot them than in the northern parks.

This low lying reserve (360 - 4,100 ft.) is composed of woodlands, grasslands, flood-plains and dense forests. It has been spared encroachment by man because the soil is too poor to farm and tsetse flies prevent grazing of domestic animals.

Walking safaris accompanied by an armed ranger are popular. Exploring the Rufiji River and nearby lakes by boat and especially running the rapids of Stiegler's Gorge by raft and crossing 350 feet above the river by cable car are other adventurous ways of exploring the reserve.

Most visitors fly into the Selous from Dar es Salaam. Access by road is difficult and only possible in the dry season. The Tanzara Railway (Dar es Salaam to Zambia) passes through the northern part of the Selous about four hours after departing Dar es Salaam, and an abundance of game is usually seen. Some travelers disembark at Fuga Halt where they are taken to the camps.

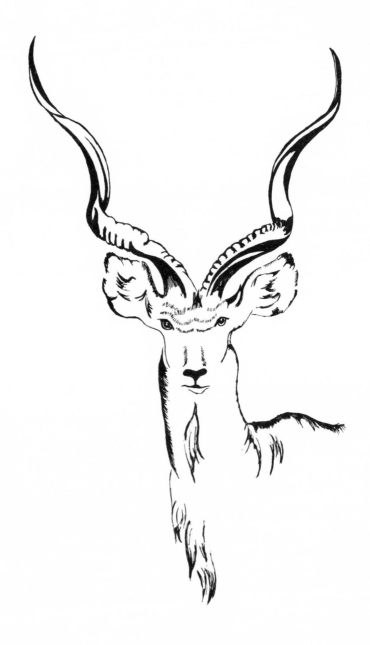

Greater Kudu

ACCOMMODATION — CLASS C: • Rufigi River Camp, basic tented camp, walking and boat safaris. • Mbuyu Safari Camp, comfortable tented camp on the Rufigi River. • Stiegler's Gorge Lodge, chalets with bathrooms, overlooks the gorge. • Selous Safari Camp, also called Beho Beho Camp, self-contained bandas.
CAMPING: Sites are available.

RUAHA NATIONAL PARK

Ruaha is one of the country's newest and best national parks, and because of its location it is one of least-visited. The Great Ruaha River with its impressive gorges runs along the park's eastern boundary and is home to many hippos and crocs. Ruaha's scenery is spectacular and its 5,000 square mile area makes it almost as large as Serengeti National Park. The landscape is characterized by rocky hills on a plateau over 3,300 feet in altitude.

The dry season June-October is the best time to visit the park when game is concentrated along the Ruaha River. Large numbers of greater kudu and elephant can be seen along with sable antelope, roan antelope, buffalo, giraffe and impala. There are a number of photographic hides (blinds) allowing close views of wildlife undisturbed by the presence of man. Park Headquarters are located at Msembe.

ACCOMMODATION — CLASS D: • Iringa Railway Hotel, in Iringa, 80 miles east of the park.
CAMPING: Campsites and self-service lodging (Class F) at Msembe. Book through the Park Warden, Ruaha National Park, P.O. Box 369, Iringa.

OTHER ATTRACTIONS

Mikumi National Park is the closest park to Dar es Salaam (185 miles) and is frequented by expatriates (foreigners working in Tanzania). This 500 square mile park is open all year although some roads are closed during the rainy season. The hippo pool is on the main highway to Zambia which divides the park.

During our two-day stay we saw elephant, zebra, six lions, giraffe, buffalo, impala, ground hornbill and guinea fowl, among other species.

ACCOMMODATION — CLASS C: ● Mikumi Wildlife Lodge.
CLASS D: ● Mikumi Wildlife Camp, self-contained bandas, restaurant and bar.
CAMPING: Campsites available.

Kigoma is the country's major port on Lake Tanganyika where you can catch a steamer to Burundi or Zambia. **Ujiji**, a small town 6 miles south of Kigoma, is where the infamous line "Dr. Livingstone, I presume" was spoken by Stanley in 1872. Accommodation (Class D) is available at the New Kigoma Railway Hotel.

Gombe Stream National Park is the setting for Jane Goodall's chimpanzee studies and her book *In the Shadow of Man*. This remote 61 square mile park is situated near Lake

Chimpanzee

Tanganyika 25 miles north of Kigoma. Other wildlife of note includes buffalo, red colobus monkeys, Defassa waterbuck and leopard.

No reservations are required. Camping is allowed; bring your own food. Accommodation available in Kigoma. The easiest access is by water taxi from a village south of Nyanza-Lac (Burundi); also by water taxi from Kigoma.

THE COAST

DAR ES SALAAM

Dar es Salaam, meaning "haven of peace", is the capital, largest city, and commercial center of Tanzania. Many safaris to the southern parks begin here. Among the more interesting sights are the harbor, National Museum, Village Museum and the Kariakoo Market.

Once the German capital, hub of the slave trade and endpoint of the slave route from the interior, **Bagamoyo** is an old seaport 46 miles north of Dar es Salaam. Fourteenth century ruins, stone pens and shackles that held the slaves may be seen.

ACCOMMODATION — FIRST CLASS: • Kilimanjaro Hotel, air-conditioned, swimming pool, fabulous view of the harbor.

TOURIST CLASS: • The New Africa Hotel, air-conditioned, popular terrace coffee shop. • Oyster Bay Hotel, 4 miles from town, excellent restaurant.

ZANZIBAR

Zanzibar and its sister island Pemba grow 75% of the world's cloves. A beautiful island unspoiled by tourism, Zanzibar is only 22 miles from the mainland — a twenty-minute flight from Dar es Salaam. A more traditional way to reach the island is a five or more hour sailing by dhow from Dar es Salaam, usually with a return to Bagamoyo.

Unlike Dar es Salaam, it is quite safe to walk around the city of Zanzibar, whose narrow streets and Arabic architecture are exceptionally mystical and beautiful on a moonlit night. Main attractions include the former British Consulate, Arab fort, Sultan's palace, Zanzibar Museum, clove market and Indian bazaar. Livingstone's and Burton's houses are near the pictur-esque Dhow Harbour.

Scheduled flights to the island are often overbooked. Customs at Zanzibar require visitors to change foreign currency on the island regardless of how much they may have previously changed on the mainland.

ACCOMMODATION — FIRST CLASS: • Oberoi Ya Bwawani Hotel, saltwater pool, disco and excellent food.

TOURIST CLASS: • Zanzibar Hotel, traditional Arabic design.

UGANDA

SUDAN

WILDLIFE AREAS
LAKE
CAPITAL
RAILROAD
TOWN

ZAIRE

NILE R.

MOROTO

GULU

PAKWACH

MURCHISON
FALLS N.P.

LAKE
ALBERT

MT. ELGON

NILE R.

FORT PORTAL

KAMPALA

TORORO

RUWENZORI
MTS.

JINJA

ENTEBBE

KENYA

LAKE GEORGE
KAZINGA
CHANNEL

LAKE
EDWARD

RUWENZORI
N.P.

L. MBORO
N.P.

LAKE
VICTORIA

KABALE

KIGEZI
MT. GORILLA
G.R.

TANZANIA

RWANDA

LAKES

FACTS AT A GLANCE

Area:	91,120 square miles
Approximate size:	Oregon
Population:	16 million (1987 est.)
Capital:	Kampala (pop. est. 350,000)
Languages:	Official: English; Swahili is widely spoken

Uganda, once the "Pearl of the British Empire" in East Africa, is one of the most beautiful countries on the continent. One-sixth of its area is covered by water. Along its western boundary lies Africa's highest mountain range, Ptolemy's fabled "Mountains of the Moon." The Ugandans claim the source of the Nile is at Jinja where it leaves Lake Victoria.

The weather in Uganda is similar to Kenya's except that Uganda's is wetter. The driest time of the year is December-February and June-July, and the wettest is from mid-March to mid-May with lighter rains in October-November.

The people are well educated and English is spoken as widely as in Kenya or Tanzania. The main religions are Christianity and Islam.

In the 18th century the Bagandan kingdom became the most powerful in the region; it was made a British Protectorate in 1893 and achieved independence in 1962. Over 90% of the population is employed in agriculture. Coffee is the major export.

The country has had more than its fair share of turmoil over the past 15 years; in spite of this, the people are among the friendliest on the continent.

Although I have traveled through many parts of Uganda and have only been met with kindness, as of this writing, travel there is still very risky. Be sure to contact the Department of State (see "Security" in The Safari Pages) for travel advisories and register with your embassy on arrival. I have included Uganda in this guide with the hope that conditions will improve.

WILDLIFE AND WILDLIFE AREAS

This country was once very rich in wildlife, but much of the larger game was killed during Idi Amin's rule and in the war to oust him in the late 1970s. However, wildlife populations are coming back. A real plus is that one seldom meets another vehicle on game drives — in essence having the park to themselves.

Uganda has four national parks and 16 reserves. The calving seasons for hartebeest and Uganda kob are January-February and for oribi, February-March.

NORTHERN AND WESTERN

MURCHISON (KABALEGA) FALLS NATIONAL PARK

This park is named after the famous falls where the Victoria Nile rushes through a narrow rock gorge 20 feet wide with tremendous force, crashing on the rocks 150 feet below. Fish dazed by this fall are easy prey to one of the largest concentrations of crocodile on the continent.

Located in northwestern Uganda, this park covers approximately 1,500 square miles of predominantly grassy plains and savannah woodlands. Riverine forest lines some parts of the Victoria Nile, which traverses the park from east to west. The Rabongo Forest has a population of chimpanzees.

Not to be missed is the three-hour, 7-mile launch trip from the Paraa Lodge to the foot of the falls. Numerous crocodiles and hippos in the river and along its banks, as well as buffalo, elephant, and prolific birdlife (over 400 species) can be approached closely. The park is also home to giraffe, waterbuck, oribi, and Uganda kob.

Park headquarters and the most extensive road system for game viewing are near the Paraa Lodge. The Buligi Circuit takes one to the confluence of the Albert and Victoria Niles. Water foul are especially abundant, along with a variety of game.

The easiest time to spot animals is January-February. From March to May the landscape is more attractive and the wildlife is less concentrated. The short dry season from June-July is also good.

Record Nile perch weighing over 200 pounds have been caught in the Nile. Some of the best fishing is just below Karuma Falls near Chobe Safari Lodge, and just below Murchison Falls.

Subject to availability and fuel, ranger's vehicles can be

Giraffe

rented with a driver/guide for game drives. Often fuel is not available for vehicles or the boat. Bring along 30 liters of diesel for the launch trip to be safe.

ACCOMMODATION — There are airstrips at all three lodges.

CLASS D: • Chobe Lodge, overlooks picturesque Victoria Nile.

CLASS F: • Paraa Lodge, in poor condition. • Pakuba Grand Lodge, situated near Pakwach.

CAMPING: Several sites available.

RUWENZORI (QUEEN ELIZABETH) NATIONAL PARK

The park is about 770 square miles of tremendous scenic variety with volcanic craters and crater lakes, grassy plains, swamps, rivers, lakes and tropical forest. The snow-capped Ruwenzori Mountains lie to the north and are not part of the park itself.

The launch trip on the Kazinga Channel which joins Lakes Edward and George affords excellent opportunities for viewing hippos and a great variety of waterfowl at close range.

The Katwe-Kirongo area in the north of the park has several saline lakes. South of the Kazinga Channel, the Maramagambo Forest is home for large numbers of chimpanzees, colobus monkeys and baboons. The Ishasha region in the south of the park is famous for its tree-climbing lions.

There are also elephant, buffalo, leopard, sitatunga, Uganda kob, topi, and waterbuck. The rare pre-historic looking whale-headed stork is often sighted along the shores of Lake George.

Interestingly enough there are no giraffe, zebra, impala or rhino, or crocodiles in the Kazinga Channel or Lakes Edward and George. The crocodiles are believed to have been killed long ago by volcanic activity.

From Kampala the park is 260 miles via Mbarara and 285 miles via Fort Portal. There is a landing strip at Mweya for light aircraft and for larger planes at Kasese. Park vehicles and guides are available for hire at park headquarters at Mweya.

ACCOMMODATION — CLASS C: • Mweya Lodge, best lodge in the country, situated on a high bluff overlooking the Kazinga Channel and Lake Edward.

CAMPING: Sites near Mweya Lodge and the Kazinga Channel.

THE RUWENZORI MOUNTAINS

This is the highest mountain range in Africa and the legendary "Mountains of the Moon." They rise 13,000 feet above the western arm of the Rift Valley just north of the equator and are usually covered in mist. See "Ruwenzori Mountains" in the chapter on Zaire for a general description.

Hikers in good condition can enjoy walking strenuous trails rising to over 13,000 feet in altitude through some of the most amazing vegetation in the world. There is a circuit with huts that takes a minimum of five days to hike — preferably six or seven. Mountain huts in very poor condition can be used without charge.

The main trailhead begins near Ibanda (about 2,950 ft.). Drive a short distance north from Kasese on the Fort Portal road, then turn left (west) for eight miles. John Maate and his son can outfit you with guides and porters. Bring all your own equipment. For additional information contact the Mountain Club of Kenya or write John Maate, P.O. Box 88, Kasese, and enclose an international reply coupon to cover their mailing costs. International reply coupons are available at most post offices.

CENTRAL AND SOUTHERN

KAMPALA

The capital of Uganda, this city is built on seven hills. Points of interest include the Uganda Museum and the Kasubi Tombs of the Kabakas — a shrine to the former Bagandan kings and a fine example of Baganda craftsmanship.

ACCOMMODATION — FIRST CLASS: • Hotel Diplomate, a good hotel — and about the only one that does not suffer chronic water shortages, fine restaurant, situated a few miles out of town.

OTHER ATTRACTIONS

Uganda's newest national park and formally a game reserve, **Lake Mburo National Park** is located in southwestern Uganda between Masaka and Mbarara. This approximately 200 square mile park is named after Lake Mburo, the largest of the fourteen lakes. The park is characterized by open plains in the north, acacia grassland in the center and lakes and marshes in the south.

Wildlife includes hippo, buffalo, zebra, eland, roan antelope, reedbuck, topi, bushbuck, and klipspringer. Impala, which do not exist in any other park in Uganda, are numerous. There are some lion and leopard. Camping sites are available in the park.

Kabale is a small town in a beautiful area called "The little Switzerland of Africa." The best accommodation (Class D) is at the White Horse Inn.

The **Kigezi Mountain Gorilla Game Reserve** is situated on the slopes of Mts. Muhabura and Gahinga in the southwestern corner of Uganda bordering Rwanda and Zaire. Across these mountains lies the Volcano National Park in Rwanda which is also famous for its gorilla population.

Gorillas are less likely to be sighted here than in the Volcano National Park in Rwanda or in Kahuzi-Biega National Park in Zaire. The Ugandan side of the mountains is dryer and provides less moisture and less vegetation which gorillas prefer to eat. However, the clearer skies provide breathtaking views of the most beautiful part of this country.

The infamous guide Zacharia has been leading groups up the mountain in search of gorillas for over 20 years. Request his services at the Traveller's Rest Hotel in Kisoro at least 24 hours in advance. Even if gorillas are not seen, the hike through this peaceful scenic region of friendly people is well worth the effort. The Traveller's Rest is the best hotel (Class D) in the area.

ZAIRE

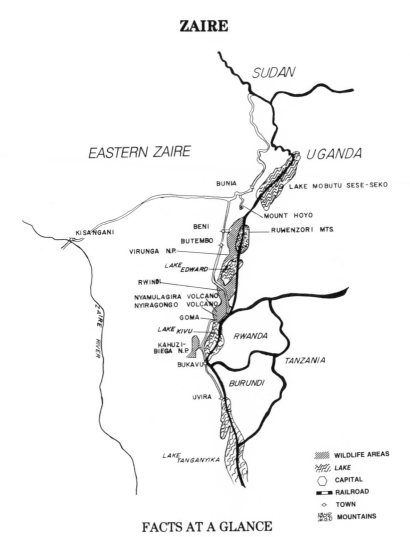

FACTS AT A GLANCE

Area:	607,400 square miles
Approximate size:	USA east of the Mississippi River
Population:	35.5 million (1987 est.)
Capital:	Kinshasa (pop. est. 3,000,000)
Languages:	Official: French. National: Swahili, Tshiluba, Kikongo and Lingala

The Republic of Zaire, formerly the Democratic Republic of the Congo, is the third-largest country in Africa. The name Zaire comes from the Kikongo word *nzadi*, meaning "river". The Congo or Zaire River, the 10th longest river in the world, winds 2,880 miles through the Zaire basin, the world's second-largest drainage basin (the Amazon is the largest), and finally empties into the Atlantic ocean.

Kivu Province, the most beautiful region of Zaire, holds the country's most exciting attractions. This province is situated along the western borders of Rwanda and Uganda in the region of the great lakes — Lakes Tanganyika, Kivu, Edward, and Mobutu (Albert).

Due to the altitude the region has an agreeable Mediterranean-type climate. In general, the best time to visit eastern Zaire is during the dry seasons from December-February and mid-June-August.

Of the 700 or so tribal or ethnic groups, 4/5ths are Bantu. About 80% of the population is Christian with the balance having Muslim or traditional beliefs.

The area remained virtually unknown until Henry Morton Stanley traveled from East Africa to the mouth of the Congo (Zaire) River from 1874-1877. The Belgian King Leopold the Second claimed what became the Congo Free State as his personal property until he ceded it to Belgium in 1907 and it was renamed the Belgian Congo. Zaire achieved independence on June 30, 1967.

Zaire is a country of gigantic untapped resources. Half of the land is arable and scarcely 2% is under cultivation or used as pasture. The country holds 13% of the world's hydroelectric potential. Copper accounts for 50% of the country's exports, followed by petroleum, diamonds and coffee.

WILDLIFE AND WILDLIFE AREAS

Eight reserves cover 15% of the country's area. Virunga National Park is one of the finest reserves in Africa and contains the world's largest concentration of hippos. Over 1,000 species of birds have been recorded in Zaire, many in the Virunga National Park.

The parks and reserves in Zaire are much less crowded than the ones in East Africa. During my latest visit, there were only four visitors staying at Virunga National Park's Rwindi Lodge and I was the only visitor to Mt. Hoyo and the Ruwenzori Mountains in two weeks. The world has not yet discovered that these are among the continent's finest attractions, making a visit here all the more inviting and adventurous.

THE NORTH

GOMA

Goma is the tourist center for eastern Zaire, and for-tunately tourism has done little to change this typical African town. A government tourist office (Centre d'Accueil du Tourisme, B.P. 242, Goma) is located on Boulevard Mobutu.
ACCOMMODATION — FIRST CLASS: • Hotel Karibu, six miles outside of Goma on Lake Kivu.
TOURIST CLASS: • The Masques Hotel, located in town, good restaurant.

NORTH OF GOMA

The drive from Goma northward one passes over the dramatic Kabasha Escarpment to Butembo. The route from the Kabasha Escarpment to Beni is one of the most beautiful in Africa and is properly named the "Beauty Route." The road passes through many picturesque villages, coffee, tea and banana plantations — the Africa that many of us have pictured in our minds.

The region around Goma is a highly volcanic area of constant activity. On my first visit here I discovered that a new volcano had recently been born, and we hiked 10 miles into the bush to see it. In case of an eruption, we camped uphill from the volcano which was scarcely 300 feet high and watched the fabulous fireworks all night. For some unknown reason a new volcano pops up in this active region about every other year between December and April. I just missed visiting another lava-filled caldera in 1984 which cooled a few weeks before my arrival.

VIRUNGA NATIONAL PARK
(PARC NATIONAL DES VIRUNGA)

Virunga National Park is the best game park in Zaire and is one of the finest and least known parks in all of Africa. With approximately 4,600 square miles in area it is one of the largest on the continent as well. Altitudes range from 3000 feet on the grassy savannah to 16,794 feet in the Ruwenzori mountains, resulting in a tremendous variety of topography, flora and fauna.

Virunga is about 185 miles long and 25 miles wide and is divided into several sections, each requiring separate entrance fees. From south to north: the Nyiragongo and Nyamulagira volcanos, gorilla reserve, Rwindi, the Ruwenzori Mountains, and Mt. Hoyo. Guides are compulsory and their services are included in the park entrance fees.

GORILLAS

Just recently gorillas may be visited here as well as in Kahuzi-Biega National Park to the south. About 30 miles north of Goma turn right and follow a rough track for another nine miles. Guides are available to take visitors to see the silverback named Marcel and his group of females and juveniles. The number of visitors is limited. If possible, reserve in advance at the Rwindi Hotel or at the tourist office in Goma.

NYIRAGONGO/NYAMULAGIRA VOLCANOS

In the southern part of the park near Goma lie the active volcanos of Nyiragongo (11,384 ft.) and Nyamulagira (10,023 ft.) which do not require technical mountaineering skills to climb. If the volcanos are active at the time of your visit, you may want to spend a night near the crater rim to enjoy the remarkable fireworks display.

Nyiragongo erupted in 1977, spewing out miles of molten

lava which destroyed villages within its path. I visited the area three months later and could still feel the heat radiating from the road which was now 30 feet higher from the flow.

Nyiragongo can be climbed in one day. Drive from Goma eight miles to the guide and porter station at Kibati (altitude of 6,400 ft.), hike 4 - 5 hours to the summit and have lunch on the crater rim. Allow 2 - 3 hours to return to Kibati. Two days may be taken for the climb, overnighting at a refuge near the summit. Bring a sleeping bag, food and water.

Nyamulagira can be climbed in two (preferably three) days. Nights are spent in a basic lodge at 8,200 feet altitude and near the crater's edge. Hike up the first day, spend the second day descending into the crater, then return on the third day. An armed guide accompanies each group, and porters may be hired. With luck you will see forest elephant, chimpanzees, buffalo and antelope. Drive to Kakomero 24 miles north of Goma. Bring your own food and gear.

The best time to climb is December - January and June when the weather is the clearest. February, July and August are also good.

RWINDI

Continuing north towards Rwindi are the Rutshuru Waterfalls and hot-water springs (*maji ya moto*) near Rutshuru.

The savannah plains and swamps surrounding Rwindi Village are the chief game viewing areas of Virunga National Park and have the greatest concentrations of hippo in the

Hippopotamus

world (about 30,000). The Kabasha Escarpment provides a dramatic backdrop for wildlife which includes elephant, buffalo, hippo, lion, hyena, jackals, waterbuck, reedbuck, bushbuck, topi, Thomas kob, Defassa kob, crocodiles and aquatic birds. During one 2-hour game drive we spotted a dozen lion and over 200 elephant, with one herd numbering over 80.

The fishing village of Vitshumbi on the southern shores of Lake Edward is where elephants can occasionally be seen roaming the streets. Visit the fishery to enjoy the taste of delicious barbecued tilapia with pilipili (hot sauce).

Most game viewing is from mini-buses with roof-hatches. Vehicles must stay on the park tracks. The main road from Goma to Butembo passes right through the park. Roads and tracks are poor in the rainy season.

Rwindi Lodge, park headquarters and camping sites are located at Rwindi, 81 miles north of Goma. Rwindi Lodge provides tourist class accommodation. Camping is allowed nearby.

RUWENZORI MOUNTAINS

The third highest mountains in Africa (behind Mts. Kilimanjaro and Kenya), the "Mountains of the Moon" are the highest mountain chain on the continent. Permanently snow-covered over 14,800 feet, these jagged mountains are almost perpetually covered in mist. The highest peak is Margherita (16,794 ft.). A number of permanent glaciers and peaks challenge mountaineers. However, mountaineering skills are not needed for the hike itself — only for climbing the glaciers or peaks.

Unlike Mt. Kilimanjaro and many other mountains in east and central Africa, the Ruwenzoris are not Volcanic in origin. The range forms part of the border with Uganda and can be climbed from either the Zaire or Ugandan side. The trail on the Zaire side of the Ruwenzoris is much steeper than the Ugandan side. Allow five days for the climb to the highest hut, and longer if any peaks are to be attempted.

The vegetation zones one passes through on the Ruwenzoris are the most amazing I have seen in the world. Colorful mosses which look solid but when probed with a walking stick (or your foot) often prove to cover a tangle of roots more than six feet thick. Several plants that are commonly small in other parts of the world grow to gigantic proportions.

Plan on walking 4 - 5 hours per day. The first day of hiking is from the park headquarters at Mutsora (5,600 ft.) to Kalonge (7,015 ft.) through small fields of bananas, coffee, and other crops.

On the second day one passes through bamboo forest, spongy mosses and heather 25 feet tall to Mahangu Hut (10,860 ft.). The third day one enters a zone of giant groundsels over 16 feet high and giant lobelia over 25 feet high to Kiondo Hut (13,780 ft.). The night I spent at Kiondo Hut was filled with spine tingling shrieks from what was only later identified as the harmless bushbaby.

That afternoon or the next morning (the fourth day) hike either to Wasuwameso for some fabulous views of Mt. Stanley

Bush Baby

or go for a three-hour round-trip hike to Moraine Hut (14,270 ft.) at the foot of the glaciers. The hike to Moraine Hut requires a short bit of easy rock climbing. Be sure to return early. I returned in the dark, and had I not brought a flashlight, my guide and I might still be up there. Return to Mutsora the afternoon of the fourth or the fifth day.

The best time to climb is from December-January and July-August; February and June are also good. Drive north through Butembo to Beni, then east 28 miles to Mutwanga. Park headquarters is at Mutsora, about 1.5 miles from Mutwanga.

A guide at no charge is required; porters are available for a small fee. The guides know the path and where to find water en route — but little else. None is equipped for or experienced in glacier or rock climbing, so your group must be self-sufficient. There are no mountain rescue teams.

Accommodation on the mountain is in dilapidated shacks with fireplaces and a few large pots for cooking. Bring your own sleeping bag, mattress, food and enough water to last two days. For accommodation before or after the climb, see Butembo below. Camping is allowed at park headquarters.

MOUNT HOYO

About 12 miles south of Komanda on the road from Beni take the track to the east, uphill for nine miles to the colonial-style Mt. Hoyo Lodge (Auberge du Mount Hoyo). I was dropped off a produce truck loaded with bananas and goats at this intersection at 2:30 one morning and hiked all night, passing Pygmy villages along the way and arriving in time for breakfast. I ventured upon a line of millions of safari ants crossing the road. Thousands of ants joined their legs and formed a "cocoon" across the road, protecting those that crossed beneath.

Mt. Hoyo has many attractions. The Cascades of Venus (Escalier de Venus) is a stepped waterfall in a thick jungle setting of natural beauty. The cascades and the grottoes (caves) with stalagmites and stalactites can be easily visited in a half-day hike. Black and white colobus monkeys, chimpanzees and the rare okapi may be seen in the forest.

For a very interesting excursion, join a few Balese (pygmy) hunters on a mock antelope hunt. Armed with bows and arrows, these hunters lead groups of up to three visitors through thick jungle vegetation in search of game. The pygmies whistle to attract their "prey." Here they proved the advantage of being short — effortlessly walking under vines and limbs while I had to crawl on my hands and knees.

We feasted on honey which they fished out of a bee hive in a tree-trunk with their arrows, and they enjoyed another delicacy — termites from a large mound.

Accommodation (Class D) is available at the Mount Hoyo Hotel (Auberge du Mt. Hoyo). Camping is allowed nearby.

OTHER ATTRACTIONS

The **Loya River** crosses the main road a few miles south of the turnoff to Mt. Hoyo. Take a ride in a piroque (dug-out canoe) through the thick green Ituri forest to authentic Ituri villages, past artificial dams created for fishing, and thick jungle.

Situated outside of the Virunga National Park in the highlands just north of the equator is the large busy village of **Butembo**. The Kikyo Hotel (Tourist Class) offers the best accommodation.

THE SOUTH

KAHUZI-BIEGA NATIONAL PARK

This 230 square mile mountain sanctuary is located 22 miles northwest of Bukavu and is dedicated to preserving gorillas. Searching for these magnificent, rare and endangered animals is recommended only for travelers in good physical condition.

The entrance to the park is at 5,900 feet and the search may take from one to five hours of hiking to an altitude of over 7,550 feet through dense upland jungle and bamboo forests. Bring good walking shoes (i.e. high-topped sneakers — not boots) since you may be wading through water, a sweater, a raincoat or other waterproof covering, lunch and canteen.

On my visit to the park I was the only tourist there to search for gorillas. I was accompanied by a guide and several cutters wielding pangas. As our search progressed we found gorilla lairs where they had spent the previous night.

After four hours of following their trail and cutting our way through dense tropical foliage we finally located them. The silverback (dominant male) was one of the largest I have ever seen — estimated by the guide to weigh over 500 pounds. Hanging vines and branches that blocked our view were cut until he pounded his chest and charged, stopping just short of us, establishing his well-earned territory. In the background an adult female and her young offspring were curiously watching.

The Frankfurt Zoological Society now manages the park, and is in the process of adopting many of the same regulations as the Volcano National Park in Rwanda. Book in advance with the tourist office (Office National du Tourisme) or through a travel agent or tour operator.

Children under 15 years of age are not allowed to visit the gorillas. In the rare event that gorillas are not sighted, visitors may return for another search without paying additional fees. The closest comfortable accommodation is in Bukavu. Tents may be rented and camping sites are available at the park headquarters.

BUKAVU

Bukavu, the region's capital, is located in a beautiful setting situated on the southern shores of Lake Kivu near the Rwandan border. A tourist office (Office National du Tourisme) is located on Avenue President Mobutu, B.P. 2468; tel. 3001.
ACCOMMODATION — TOURIST CLASS: • Hotel Residence, finest hotel in the region, very good French cuisine.

CENTRAL AND WESTERN

ZAIRE RIVER

Exploring the Zaire River by ferry from Kinshasa to Kisangani is truly an adventure into the dark continent. The boat is slow, taking about 10 days upstream and six downstream for the 1000 mile voyage, if no complications arise. Local tribesmen paddle out to meet the riverboat in their dugout canoes, latch hold and sell monkeys, crocodiles, huge juicy pineapples and other tropical fruits, then float back downstream to their village. One passes through the "mainstream" of Zairian life on this river. First class is recommended for all but the most rugged of travelers.

KINSHASA

Situated in western Zaire on the Congo (Zaire) River, Kinshasa is the country's capital and one of the most expensive cities in the world. Points of interest include the Presidential Gardens and Zoo, the central market, and the National Academy of Fine Arts.
ACCOMMODATION — DELUXE: Inter-Continental Hotel.
FIRST CLASS: Hotel le Memling.

WILLIFE AREAS
LAKE
CAPITAL
RAILROAD
TOWN

FACTS AT A GLANCE

Area: 290,585 square miles
Approximate size: Texas
Population: 7 million (1987 est.)
Capital: Lusaka (pop. est. 600,000)
Languages: Official: English

This sparsely populated country is rich in wildlife and was named after the mighty Zambezi River flowing through the south of Zambia, fed by its Kafue and Luangwa tributaries. The three great lakes of Bangweulu, Mweru and Tanganyika lie in the north of Zambia and Lake Kariba lies along the south-eastern border with Zimbabwe.

The country is predominantly a high plateau ranging in altitude from 3,000-5,000 feet, which is why it has a subtropical rather than a tropical climate. April-August is cool and dry, September-October is hot and dry, and November-March is warm and wet. Winter temperatures are as cool as 43° F and summer temperatures as warm as 100° F. The dry season, with clear sunny skies, occurs May-October.

The Zambian people are predominantly composed of Bantu tribal groups who practice a combination of traditional and Christian beliefs. English is the official language and is widely spoken. About 70 other languages and dialects are also spoken. In contrast to most African countries, over 40% of the population lives in urban areas, due mainly to the copper mining industry.

Cecil Rhodes obtained mineral right concessions from the chiefs in 1888 in what was proclaimed Northern Rhodesia, which came under British influence. In 1953 Northern Rhodesia, Southern Rhodesia and Nyasaland (now Malawi) were consolidated into the Federation of Rhodesia and Nyasaland. Northern Rhodesia seceded from the Federation in 1963 and achieved its independence on October 24, 1964 as the Republic of Zambia.

Zambia's economy is based primarily on copper from the government owned mines in the "copper belt" near the Zaire border, the price and subsequent production of which has declined since 1975 and has brought on hardship and forced the economy to diversify.

WILDLIFE AND WILDLIFE AREAS

Zambia boasts 19 gazetted National Parks covering over 24,500 square miles, and with the 34 Game Management Areas adjacent to the parks, Zambia has set aside 32% of its land to the preservation of wildlife. However, many national parks and reserves are not open to the general public.

Zambia's two major parks are South Luangwa National Park and Kafue National Park. South Luangwa is the more popular of the two, largely due to its high concentration of elephant and other game. In Kafue National Park the game is generally more scattered, but many of the species such as greater kudu and sable antelope are said to be substantially larger than elsewhere in the country. The red lechwe, unique to Zambia, is found in Kafue.

Going on safari in Zambia is different. In Kenya and Tanzania visitors are often rushed from park to park with only one or two nights in the same park. In Zambia the emphasis is on experiencing the bush and wildlife by participating in walking safaris (the biggest attraction), night safaris and boat safaris. A tour of Zambia should consist of a visit to Victoria Falls and one national park (preferably South Luangwa, with Kafue National Park as a second choice). A long visit could, of course, include both parks.

Zambia is the best country to visit for walking safaris, which are operated in South Luangwa (my first choice) and Kafue (my second choice) National Parks. Groups of usually up to six adults (children under 12 are not allowed) are accompanied by an armed wildlife guard on slow-paced safaris of 2-6 days in length, overnighting in simple but comfortable camps (often chalets). Luggage and provisions are carried ahead to the next camp by vehicles using a different route from the walks. Wildlife is tracked just as in a hunting safari except game is "shot" with a camera instead of a gun. Since more wildlife is usually seen from a vehicle, a combination of walking and vehicle safaris is advised.

Most of the lodges and camps offer game viewing drives. Open vehicles are allowed, and game drives with spotlights at night may be conducted by the camps.

Fishing for tiger fish, lake salmon and Nile perch is excellent in Lake Tanganyika, Lake Kariba, and the Kafue River, and is best April to November.

Visitors who have their own vehicles must be in the camps by nightfall, must not leave the roads in search of game or walk in the park without the company of an armed wildlife guard. I've been told that crocodiles in Zambia are responsible for more deaths than automobile accidents.

THE NORTH

SOUTH LUANGWA NATIONAL PARK

The natural beauty, variety and concentration of wildlife make this huge 3,500 square mile park one of the finest in Africa. Game is prolific (Luangwa is called "The Crowded Valley"), with one of the highest concentrations of elephant on the continent. Unfortunately the effects of this large elephant population are evident as many woodlands have been devastated.

Elephant

The park is home to savannah, wetland and forest animals. The southern regions are predominantly woodland savannah with scattered grassy areas. Leopard, kudu and giraffe are numerous. To the north the woodlands give way to scattered trees and open plains where wildebeest and other savannah animals dominate the scene.

Thornicroft's giraffe and the rare white impala are indigenous to the park. Lion, hyena, buffalo, waterbuck, impala, kudu, puku and zebra are plentiful. Small herds of Cookson's wildebeest may be seen. This is the best park in Zambia to see hippo completely out of the water. Leopard are most commonly sighted July-October. Black rhino are present but infrequently seen.

Over 400 species of birds have been recorded, including sacred ibis, saddle bill storks, yellow bill storks, Egyptian geese, spurwinged geese, fish eagles, crested cranes and long-tailed starlings. Hippos and crocs abound in the muddy Luangwa River, a tributary of the Zambezi which runs along much of the park's eastern boundary and then traverses the southern part of the park.

Near Mfuwe Lodge we saw lion, a pack of 21 African wild dogs, civet, buffalo, wildebeest, waterbuck, greater kudu, puku, impala, crocs, hippos mating and fighting, Thornicroft's giraffes, elephant, zebra, monitor lizard, warthog, and the ever-present baboons and vervet monkeys. Just before sunrise, elephants can sometimes be seen crossing the Luangwa River.

There are few all-weather roads in the park north of Mfuwe, so most of the northern camps are closed from November-April. The best time to visit is September, followed by July. In August there are many European visitors; October-May is the hot and humid rainy season when foliage becomes thicker making wildlife more difficult to spot; in June the grass is still high; July is good but a bit crowded. Walking safaris are usually conducted only June-October.

Mfuwe Airport is about a one hour and fifteen minute flight from Lusaka while the drive takes about 10 hours.

ACCOMMODATION IN SOUTHERN SOUTH LUANGWA (Open Year Round) — CLASS B: Kapani Safari Camp, operated by Norman Carr who introduced walking safaris to Zambia. Chalets with full facilities, veranda and refrigerator, swimming pool, bar, restaurant. Walking safaris June-October.

Warthog

CLASS C: • Mfuwe Lodge, on a picturesque lagoon teeming with hippo and crocs, rooms with bath, good restaurant, bar, swimming pool, shop. • Chichele Lodge modern design, set high on a hill overlooking the Luangwa River, rooms with toilet and shower, most with a/c, restaurant, bar. • Chinzombo Safari Lodge, on the eastern bank of the Luangwa River across from the park. Profits go to the "Save the Rhino Trust."

ACCOMMODATION IN NORTHERN SOUTH LUANGWA (open May-October) — CLASS C: • Chibembe, fully-catered camp just outside the northeastern boundary of the park on the Luangwa River, rooms with showers and toilets, swimming pool. Walking safaris, no vehicle game drives. • Nsefu Camp, offers driving and walking safaris.

CAMPING: Not allowed in the park.

SUMBU NATIONAL PARK

Sumbu National Park borders the huge inland sea of Lake Tanganyika in the extreme north of Zambia. Visitors come to this 780 square mile park for game viewing, fishing and water sports. The lake in this area is reputedly bilharzia-free; be sure to check for its current status.

Forest and wetland wildlife species are plentiful. In fact, visitors are often accompanied to the sandy beaches by wildlife guards. Elephant, lion, and a variety of antelope may be seen while game viewing by vehicle or by boat. The shoreline is inhabited by hippos, crocodiles and water birds. Savannah dominates the park inland.

Fishing for goliath tiger fish, vundu (giant catfish), lake salmon and Nile Perch in Lake Tanganyika is excellent, especially November-March. Boats are available for hire. Quickest access is by air from Lusaka.

ACCOMMODATION — CLASS C: Kasaba Bay Lodge, near Lake Tanganyika. Ndole Bay, located just outside the park.

THE SOUTH

LUSAKA

Lusaka is capital of Zambia. Sights include the Luburma Market and Munda Wanga Botanical Garden and Zoological Park.

ACCOMMODATION — DELUXE: • Pamodzi Hotel, a/c, restaurant, coffee shop, four bars, swimming pool, nightly entertainment, 24 hour room service, tour packages. • Lusaka Inter-Continental Hotel, a/c, 3 restaurants, casino, swimming pool.

FIRST CLASS: • Ridgeway Hotel, a/c, rooms with bath, restaurant, swimming pool.

KAFUE NATIONAL PARK

Kafue National Park is one of the largest in Africa, covering 8650 square miles making it 2½ times the size of South Luangwa National Park. Game is more difficult to see here than in South Luangwa as much of Kafue, especially the southern areas, is clothed with a double-canopy forest.

The southern and central parts are open all year while the northern areas are only open during the dry season June-November. Game is especially difficult to spot in the rainy season.

Game drives in this park are often a combination of riding in a vehicle and walking, according to the wishes of the group.

On daylight game drives in the south of the park we found buffalo, elephant, zebra, impala, warthog, hippo, sable antelope, zebra, wildebeest and buffalo. By air we spotted several illegal fisherman's huts on an island in the lake. Lion are also seen.

Night game drives produced sightings of impala, oribi, hundreds of spring hares, greater kudu, buffalo, serval, bushbuck, duiker, spotted hyena, zebra, elephant, Defassa waterbuck and bushbabies.

Lake Itezhi-Tezhi, formed as the result of a hydro-electric dam constructed at the southern end of the Kafue Flats, provides fishing and boating opportunities for visitors.

On a motorboat ride on the Kafue River we passed numerous fishermen, several small villages, crocodiles, hippo, many magnificent fish eagles, spurwinged geese, pied kingfishers, herons, sacred ibis, Egyptian geese, egrets, and river monitors.

We went further along the river than most visitors go and found men transporting hippo meat in several canoes. Upon

Defassa Waterbuck

our return to Musungwa Lodge we reported the incident to the manager, who immediately took two park rangers in the lodge's boat (the park has no vehicles or boats of its own) to where we had seen them. The poacher was arrested. Such cooperation of private enterprise with government conservation efforts is highly commendable.

On a drive from Musungwa to Nanzhila Camp in the southern part of the park we saw hundreds of elephant with one herd numbering over 40, scattered zebra, sable, Lichtenstein's hartebeest, and wildebeest, plentiful reedbuck and oribi, and huge herds of buffalo numbering in the thousands. On our return to Musungwa we were stuck in the mud for 1½ hours which delayed us sufficiently to allow another opportunity for a night game drive.

The Busanga Plains and marshes in the north have a greater number and variety of wildlife species which are easier to spot than those in the dense woodland savannah of the south. This region is characterized by mopane and miomo forests, rock hills, open plains, marches and riverine forests. The Kafue River runs through the northern part of the park and along its east central border.

Leopard and cheetah are seen on the Busanga Plains, as are large herds of rare red lechwe. Buffalo, elephant, puku, wildebeest impala, roan, sable, kudu and waterbuck are also present. The Kafue Flats are an excellent location to spot many of the park's more than 400 recorded species of birds.

There is little to be seen on the three hour, 170 mile drive from Lusaka, so those with limited time may wish to charter a plane.

ACCOMMODATION IN SOUTHERN KAFUE — CLASS B: • Musungwa Safari Lodge, most comfortable accommodation in the park area, just outside the eastern boundary of the park. Comfortable rooms, some with private facilities, good food and service, attractive pool and veranda. Sunset cruises, river trips, game drives.

CLASS C: • Ngoma Lodge, two rooms share facilities, swimming pool, airstrip.

ACCOMMODATION IN NORTHERN KAFUE — CLASS C: The following four camps specialize in walk-ride safaris. Most chalets have private showers and toilets. Camps are open May-October. • Moshi Camp, situated on a hill; • Ntemwa, most northern river side camp; • Kafwala, overlooking Kafwala Rapids; • Lufupa, situated in the center of the northern region.

LIVINGSTONE

Livingstone is a small town of about 80,000 inhabitants 3 miles from Victoria Falls. Driving from Lusaka takes 5-6 hours and flying about 80 minutes.

The Livingstone Museum is the National Museum of Zambia and is renowned for its collection of Dr. Livingstone's memoirs. Other exhibits cover the art and culture of Zambia. The Maramba Cultural Center exhibits bandas from various districts in Zambia and presents colorful two-hour costumed performances by Zambian dancers.

The "Sunset" or "Booze Cruise" departs from the Rainbow National Lodge and is very pleasant; hippos and crocodiles are often seen. Fishing for tigerfish on the Zambia River is best from June-October (September is ideal) before the rains muddy the waters.

Livingstone Zoological Park is a small fenced park near Livingstone covering 25 square miles; it is stocked with greater kudu, white rhino, impala, and other wildlife. The best time to visit is from June to October.

MOSI-OA-TUNYA NATIONAL PARK (VICTORIA FALLS)

Called Mosi-oa-Tunya (the smoke that thunders), Victoria Falls should not be missed (see Zimbabwe for details on the falls). Visitors may walk along the Knife Edge Bridge for a good view of the Eastern Cataract and Boiling Pot. Air and bus service is available from Lusaka.

The Zambezi River below Victoria Falls is one of the most exciting **white-water rafting** experiences in the world. Numerous fifth-class rapids (the highest class runable) make this one of the most challenging rivers on earth. One and seven-day white-water rafting trips are operated by Sobeck on the Zambezi River below Victoria Falls.

The one-day trip is rated as the wildest commercially-run one-day trip in the world. Rafts with up to eight riders and one oarsperson disappear from sight as they drop into deep holes and crash into waves over 12 feet high, being further dwarfed by sheer cliffs often rising hundreds of feet on both sides of the canyon.

Hippos and crocs are more frequently seen further downstream. Klipspringer and other wildlife can be seen on the banks, especially during the dry season.

Camp is made on sandy riverbanks, and all meals are prepared by the staff. This trip is not for those who wish to be pampered as there are no facilities en route.

ACCOMMODATION — FIRST CLASS: • Mosi-o-Tunya Inter-Continental Hotel, a five-minute walk from Victoria Falls, a/c, swimming pool, three restaurants.

TOURIST CLASS: • Rainbow National Lodge, in Mosi-oa-Tunya National Park, traditional-style huts, restaurant.

ZIMBABWE

FACTS AT A GLANCE

Area:	151,000 square miles
Approximate size:	California
Population:	8.8 million (1987 est.)
Capital:	Harare (pop. est. 800,000)
Languages:	Official: English. Other: Shona and Sindebele

Thought by some to be the land of King Solomon's mines, Zimbabwe (previously called Rhodesia) is a country blessed with good farmland, mineral wealth, beautiful and varied landscapes, and excellent game parks.

Most of Zimbabwe consists of a central plateau 3,000-4,000 feet above sea level. The highvelt, or high plateau, stretches from southwest to northeast from 4,000-5,000 feet with a mountainous region along the eastern border from 6,000-8,000 feet in altitude. The Zambezi River runs along the northwestern border and the Limpopo River along the southern border.

The climate is moderate and seasons are reversed from the northern hemisphere. Winter days (May-August) are generally dry and sunny with day temperatures averaging 59 - 68° F. Summer daytime temperatures average 77 - 86° F with October being the hottest month. The rainy season is November-March.

The major ethnic groups are the Mashona and Matabele. About 50% of the population is syncretic (part Christian and part traditional beliefs), 25% Christian, 24% traditional, and 1% Hindu and Muslim. English is understood by about half of the population.

In the first century A.D. the region was inhabited by hunters related to the Bushmen. Cecil Rhodes and the British South Africa Company took control in 1889 and the area was named Southern Rhodesia, which became a British Colony in 1923. Unilateral Declaration of Independence (UDI) from Britain was declared by Prime Minister Ian Smith and a majority of the white settlers on November 11, 1965. Zimbabwe became officially independent on April 18, 1980.

Zimbabwe has one of the most widely diversified economies in Africa, consisting of industry, mining and agriculture (in which they are self-sufficient). Main foreign exchange earners are tobacco, minerals and tourism.

WILDLIFE AND WILDLIFE AREAS

Zimbabwe has excellent and well-maintained parks and reserves, with Victoria Falls as the premier attraction. Hwange is the country's top game park, followed by Mana Pools and Matusadona National Parks.

Reservations for all national park accommodation, camping and caravan sites can be booked through the National Parks Central Booking Office, P.O. Box 8151, Causeway; tel: Harare 706077. Information concerning the national parks can be obtained from the Zimbabwe Tourist Development Corporation (ZTDC) or from the Department of National Parks, P.O. Box 8365, Harare; tel: 707624.

THE NORTH

HARARE

Formerly called Salisbury, Harare is the capital and largest city. It is one of the cleanest and most modern cities on the continent. Points of interest in Harare include the National Museum, National Art Gallery and the Tobacco Auction. Nearby are the Larvon Bird Gardens, the Ewanrigg Botanical Gardens and Lake McIlwaine Game Park.

A beautiful park adjacent to the Monomatapa Hotel features a large variety of brilliantly colored flora. During our visit, the park featured a children's section with displays of nursery rhymes including a white Snow White and seven black dwarfs.

Harare's best restaurants include The 12,000 Horsemen, Tiffany's, The Bird and Bottle, La Fontaine, and The Bamboo Inn. Pino's Restaurant is famous for its fresh prawns from Mozambique.

ACCOMMODATION — DELUXE: • Sheraton Hotel, new five-star hotel. • Meikles Hotel, swimming pool, traditional old world atmosphere. • Monomotapa Hotel, deluxe rooms with refrigerators and a good view of the park, two cocktail bars and wine bar, three fine restaurants, swimming pool. • Jameson Hotel, very comfortable.

TOURIST CLASS: ● Ambassador Hotel, good restaurant and service.

THE WEST

HWANGE NATIONAL PARK

Hwange (previously called Wankie) is Zimbabwe's largest national park and famous for its large herds of elephant. Other predominant species include buffalo, giraffe, zebra, wildebeest, sable, white and black rhino. This is also one of the best parks on the continent to see tsessebe.

Hwange is slightly larger than the state of Connecticut, covering 5,600 square miles. The park is located in the northwest corner of the country just south of the main road between Bulawayo and Victoria Falls. Hwange boasts over 100 species of animals and 400 species of birds.

The park ranges from semi-desert in the south to mountains and a plateau in the north. The northern part of Hwange is mudstone and basalt and the southern part is Kalahari sand veld. The park has an average altitude of 3,300 feet. Winter nights can drop to below freezing and summer days can be over 100° F, while average temperatures range from 65 - 83° F.

There are no rivers and only a few streams in the north of the park, but boreholes (wells) provide sources of water year-round for wildlife. During the dry season these permanent waterholes provide an excellent stage for guests to view wildlife performing day-to-day scenes of survival.

There are no seasonal animal migrations to speak of. The best time to see wildlife is during the dry season from August-October when the game concentrates near permanent water. Game viewing is fair from June-July and in November, and poor during the rainy season from December-May when the game is widely dispersed.

Hwange has 300 miles of roads, some of which are closed during the rainy season. Vehicles must keep to the roads and visitors are not allowed to leave their vehicles except at the hides and at fenced-in picnic sites. All-weather roads run through most of the park. Some roads are tarmac which detracts a bit from the feeling of being in the bush. Vehicles with roof hatches or open roofs are allowed in the park but completely open vehicles are not, except for guests of Makalolo Camp.

There are three national park camps (Classes C/D): Main Camp, Sinamatella Camp and Robins Camp, all of which have lodge accommodation, caravan and camping sites. An airstrip is available for small aircraft at Main Camp. The closest train station is Dete Station, 15 miles from Main Camp. UTC offers a transfer service.

Main Camp is the largest camp (118 beds) and is located in the northeastern part of the park. It is open year-round and has a small grocery store and park headquarters.

Game viewing is usually very good within 10 miles of Main Camp. Wildlife commonly seen nearby includes elephant, giraffe, zebra, greater kudu, impala, buffalo, sable, wildebeest, tsessebe, black-backed jackal, lion, hyena, and cheetah. We saw a very large male lion with a full mane guarding a buffalo kill, while a jackal was darting in and out snatching morsels as dozens of vultures waited their turn.

Moonlight game viewing occurs from one or two nights before and after a full moon, when park staff escort guests to the Nyamandhlovu (meat of the elephant) Platform near Main Camp.

Sinamatella Camp is situated in the northern part of the park on a small plateau affording unobstructed views, and overlooks a waterhole frequented by elephant in the afternoon. It has 55 two-bedroom cottages and is open year-round. This is a good area for kudu, elephant, giraffe, impala, hippo, klipspringer, warthog, lion, hyena and leopard.

Robins Camp is located in the northwestern part of the park, only 75 miles from Victoria Falls, and is known for its large lion population. It is open May-October and has two and four-bedded chalets. Species often seen include impala (which attract the lion), buffalo, kudu, sable, roan, waterbuck, elephant, giraffe, reedbuck, tsessebe, lion, side-striped jackal,

Side-Striped Jackal

cheetah and hyena.

OTHER ACCOMMODATIONS — CLASS B: • Hwange Safari Lodge, borders Hwange National Park, swimming pool, elevated game viewing platform with bar, Bush camp, game drives.

CLASS C: • Makalolo, tented camp in the park. • Sikumi Tree Lodge, on a private reserve near the park. Both Makalolo and Sikumi Tree Lodge are small bush camps; guests explore the area by open vehicle and on foot with armed guards.

VICTORIA FALLS

Dr. David Livingstone became the first white man to see the Victoria Falls on November 16, 1855, and named them after his queen. In his journal he wrote, "On sights as beautiful as this, Angels in their flight must have gazed."

Victoria Falls is twice the height of Niagara Falls and one and one-half times as wide. It is divided into five separate waterfalls: Devil's Cataract, Main Falls, Horseshoe Falls, Rainbow Falls and Eastern Cataract, ranging in height from 200-355 feet. The falls are approximately 5,600 feet across.

Peak flood waters usually occur around mid-April when 150 million gallons per minute crash onto the rocks below spraying water up to 1,650 feet in the air. At this time (March-April) so much water is falling that the spray makes it difficult to see the falls. December-February is actually a better time to see them, keeping in mind that they are spectacular any time of the year.

Victoria Falls and the Zambezi River form the border between Zambia and Zimbabwe. The banks of the 1,675 mile Zambezi River are lined with thick riverine forest. The Zambezi is the only major river in Africa to flow into the Indian Ocean. Daytime and sundowner cruises operate above the falls where hippo and crocs may be spotted and elephant and other wildlife may be seen coming to the shore to drink.

Fortunately the area around the falls has not been commercialized, and there are unobstructed views from many vantage points connected by paved paths. Be prepared to get wet as you walk through a luxuriant rain forest surrounding the falls which has grown as a result of the continuous spray. A path called the Chain Walk descends from near Livingstone's statue into the gorge of the Devil's Cataract providing an excellent vantage point.

The "Flight of Angels," a flight over the falls in a small plane, is highly recommended to acquire a feeling for the true majesty of the falls. Game viewing flights upstream from the falls along the Zambezi River and over Victoria Falls National Park are also available.

Spencer's Creek Crocodile Ranch has specimens up to 14½ feet in length and weighing up to 980 pounds. The Craft Village in the middle of town is very interesting with living quarters and other structures representing traditional Zimbabwean life from the country's major tribes. Big Tree is a giant baobab over 50 feet in circumference, 65 feet high and 1,000-1,500 years old. Traditional dancing is best seen at the Victoria Falls Hotel.

The falls can also be viewed from Zambia. Zambian visas are available at the border but in case of change it is better to obtain a visa in advance.

Generally speaking, the falls are more impressive and the

Sable Antelope

accommodations and tourism infrastructure is better on the Zimbabwean side. However, one may find better bargains for souvenirs (especially wood carvings) in Zambia.

The **Victoria Falls National Park** includes the falls and a game reserve covering 215 square miles which is best known for sable antelope. Among other species are white rhino, elephant, zebra, eland, buffalo, giraffe, lion, kudu and waterbuck. There are 30 sites along the river for picnicking and fishing (beware of crocodiles). Since the game reserve does not have all-weather roads it is usually closed during the rains from November 1-May 1.

Fishing is very good for tigerfish, tilapia, and giant vundu (giant catfish). Canoe safaris on the upper Zambezi from near Kazungula (Botswana) to Victoria Falls are offered from June-October. One and seven-day white-water rafting trips are available August-December (see chapter on Zambia for details).

ACCOMMODATION — CLASS A: • Victoria Falls Hotel, the epitome of British colonial elegance, spacious terraces, colorful gardens, rooms with a/c, swimming pool, tennis courts. • Makasa Sun Hotel, modern, a/c, casino, swimming pool, tennis courts.

CLASS B: • A'Zambezi River Lodge, one of the largest buildings under traditional thatch on the continent, 1½ miles from town, congenial African atmosphere, swimming pool, a/c, rooms with private facilities, very good food.

CAMPING: • Victoria Falls Rest and Caravan Park, small hostel, camping and caravan sites.

LAKE KARIBA REGION

Sunsets over the deep blue waters of Lake Kariba dotted with islands are rated among the most spectacular in the world. This is one of the largest man-made lakes on earth covering 2,000 square miles, formed by damming the Zambezi River in 1961. The lake is 180 miles long and up to 20 miles in width, and is surrounded for the most part by untouched wilderness.

When the dam was completed and the waters in the valley began to rise, animals were forced to higher ground which quickly became islands soon to be submerged under the new lake. To save these helpless animals Operation Noah was organized by Rupert Fothergill. Over 5,000 animals, including 35 different mammal species, numerous elephant and 44 black rhinos were rescued and released in what are now Matusadona National Park and the Chete Safari Area.

Fishing is excellent for tigerfish, giant vundu, bream, cheesa and nkupi. October is the optimum month for tiger fishing and November-April are the best months for bream. Birdlife is prolific — especially waterfowl.

MATUSADONA NATIONAL PARK

Situated on the southern shore of Lake Kariba and bounded on the east by the dramatic Sanyati Gorge, this scenic 600 square mile park has an abundance of elephant, kudu, impala and buffalo — especially along the shoreline in the dry season (May-September). Other game includes lion, sable, roan, waterbuck and white rhino.

Game viewing by boat near shore and walking safaris are popular. Open landrovers are used. Fishing is excellent but beware of crocodiles.

ACCOMMODATION — CLASS B: • Bumi Hills, on the western outskirts of the park, game drives, cruises, houseboats for rent. • Fothergill Island Safari Camp, off Matusadona National Park, comfortable Batonka lodge with private facilities, game viewing on foot and by boat. • Spurwing Island, comfortable cabins and tents.

MANA POOLS NATIONAL PARK

Mana Pools National Park is situated on the southern side of the Zambezi River downstream (northeast) of Lake Kariba. During the dry season this park has one of the highest concentrations of wildlife on the continent.

This 965 square mile park is uniquely characterized by fertile river terraces reaching from the slow-moving Zambezi River inland for several miles. Small ponds and pools such as Chine Pool and Long Pool were formed as the river's course slowly drifted northwards. Reeds, sandbanks, and huge mahogany and acacia trees near the river give way to dense mopane woodland which extends to the park's southern boundary along the steep Zambezi Escarpment.

Roan Antelope

Mana Pools National Park covers part of the Middle Valley which is home for 12,000 elephant, 16,000 buffalo (herds of over 500 each), and the country's largest population of black rhino.

Species commonly seen in the park include kudu, zebra, eland, impala, bushbuck, lion, leopard, jackal, hyena and crocodile. Large schools of hippo are sometimes seen lying on the sandbanks soaking up the morning sun. Occasionally spotted are wild dog, cheetah, and the rare nyala. Large varieties of both woodland and water birds are present.

Canoe safaris from below the Kariba Dam drift downstream for up to 159 miles past Mana Pools to Kanyemba near the Mozambique border, providing excellent game viewing opportunities.

The best time to visit the park for one of the finest exhibitions of wildlife on the continent is at the end of the dry season (October) when elephant, buffalo, waterbuck and impala come to the river by the thousands to drink and graze on the lush grasses along its banks. Game viewing is also very good August-September and good June-July. Road access to the park is closed during the rainy season from November 1-April 30, during which the park can only be visited by canoe or boat on the Zambezi River.

ACCOMMODATION — CLASS B: These camps offer boat safaris, walking safaris, and use open landrovers. • Chikwenya Camp, thatched lodges on the eastern border of the park. Rukomeshe Camp, located outside the park on its western boundary, comfortable bungalows.

CAMPING: Sites available.

THE SOUTH

GREAT ZIMBABWE RUINS

The Great Zimbabwe Ruins were first discovered by settlers in 1898 and their origin is still not clear. These impressive stone ruins, located 11 miles from Masvingo, look distinctly out of place in sub-Saharan Africa where most all traditional structures have been built of mud, cow dung, straw and reeds.

This city was at its prime from the thirteenth to the fifteenth centuries A.D. The Acropolis or Hill Complex, traditionally the king's residence, is situated high on a granite hill overlooking the Temple (a walled enclosure) and the less complete restoration of the Valley complex.

The Great Zimbabwe Hotel is a fine country hotel (Class C) located a few minutes walk from the ruins, with swimming pool, good food and service, and comfortable rooms.

Impala

BULAWAYO

Bulawayo is the second-largest city in Zimbabwe and holds the National Museum and Railway Museum — both well worth a visit.
ACCOMMODATION — FIRST CLASS: The Bulawayo Sun.

MOTOPOS NATIONAL PARK

Hundreds of kopjes supporting thousands of precariously-balanced rocks give the Motopos National Park one of the most unusual landscapes in Africa. The park is divided into two sections — a general recreational area where pony trails are very popular and a game reserve. We walked near two white rhino and a baby which were eventually scared off when a herd of wildebeest stampeded nearby. Leopard and jackal are the only predators.

Cecil Rhodes was buried on a huge rock kopje called "View of the World" from which one has sensational panoramas of the rocky, barren countryside.

Hundreds of rock paintings have been discovered throughout the park. Nswatugi Cave rock paintings include images of giraffe and antelope. For Bambata Cave rock paintings allow 1½ hours for the hike. White Rhino Shelter rock paintings are also worth a visit.
ACCOMMODATIONS — FIRST CLASS: see Bulawayo.
CAMPING: Camping and bungalows (Class D) available in the park.

ADDITIONAL DESTINATIONS

BURUNDI

A little larger than the state of Vermont covering only 10,750 square miles and with a population of 5 million (1987 est.), Burundi is one of the poorest and most densely populated countries in Africa. At present Burundi is visited more by international tourists in transit than as a destination in itself. However, there are some attractions that warrant a few days stay, especially for ornithologists.

French and Kirundi are the official languages. At the better hotels and restaurants some English-speaking staff are available to assist travelers.

WILDLIFE AND WILDLIFE AREAS

All of Burundi's national parks and reserves are less than five years old. They lack access roads, camping sites and other facilities. Hunting is forbidden throughout the country.

Burundi's premier wildlife attraction is chimpanzees, along with crested mangabeys and red colobus monkeys. Other wildlife includes buffalo, several species of antelope, hyena, serval, wild cats, monkeys, baboons, a wide variety of birdlife and over 400 species of fish in Lake Tanganyika, more than most any other body of water in the world. Hippo and crocs are present in Lake Tanganyika, the Rusizi and Ruvubu Rivers. The combination of varying altitude and water create a wide range of micro-climates giving rise to a great variety of flora.

The National Institute for the Conservation of Nature (INCN) has recently created three national parks (Rusizi, Kibira, and Ruvubu) and Lake Rwihinda Nature Reserve.

BUJUMBURA

Founded in 1896 by the Germans, Bujumbura is the capital

city, major port and commercial center of Burundi with a population of 15,000. The city has excellent French and Greek restaurants. Restaurants/bars on Lake Tanganyika include Cercle Nautique, Monastere and Safari Beach. Cercle Nautique has boats for rent.

Accommodation includes Meridien Source du Nil (Deluxe), Golden Tulip Hotel du Lac Tanganyika (First Class), and Hotel Paguidas-Haidemenos and the Hotel Burundi-Palace (Tourist Class).

INLAND

The people outside Bujumbura seldom see tourists and are very friendly. Try to visit a village on market day to get a feeling of daily life in Burundi.

The best area to look for chimpanzees, red colobus and crested mangabeys is in the Kibira Forest in the **Parc National de la Kibira**, situated to the north and northeast of Bujumbura.

The northeastern region is characterized by a number of lakes and marshes covered with papyrus swamps and is known as the "Country of the Birds." The **Lake Rwihinda Nature Reserve** and the other lakes in the northern part of the country, approximately 120 miles from Bujumbura, are called the "Lakes of the Birds" and include Lakes Cohoha, Rweru, Kanzigiri and Gacamirinda; they are a birdwatcher's paradise. These lakes can be explored by barge or canoe.

Wildlife in the Ruvubu basin and **Parc National de la Ruvubu** includes hippo, crocs, leopard, antelope, monkeys and some lion.

En route to Gitega one passes **Muramvya**, the ancient city of the king and royal capital, and an active market at Bugarama. **Gitega**, the former colonial capital, is situated on the central plateau in the middle of the country, and is the second largest city. Sights include the National Museum, fine arts school, and beer market. The artistic center of **Giheta**, 7 miles from Gitega, sells wood carvings, leather goods, baskets, ceramics and ivory. The southernmost possible source of the Nile is at **Rutovu**, about 60 miles from Gitega.

LESOTHO

Lesotho is called the "Kingdom in the Sky" and has the highest lowest altitude of any country in the world. The lowest point is 4,530 feet above sea level, higher than the lowest point of any other country; most of the country lies above 6,000 feet. Lesotho is an "island" surrounded by the Republic of South Africa which makes it one of only three countries in the world (including the Vatican and the Republic of San Marino) surrounded by one other country.

The country is called Lesotho, an individual is called Masotho, and the people Basotho. The official languages are Sesotho and English, which is widely spoken. Lesotho has a population of 1.6 million (1987 est.) and is about 11,700 square miles is area — about the size of the state of Maryland.

Many men wear multi-colored traditional blankets to keep them warm in the cool and often freezing air, and wear a conical basket hat that is so representative of the country it is part of the national flag.

The Basotho are the only Africans to adapt to below-freezing temperatures that can drop to —8° F. Snow can fall in the mountains any time of the year and in the lowlands between March and September. Summer temperatures seldom rise over 90° F. The rainy season is during the summer with 85% of the annual rainfall occurring October-April. The best time to visit is November-March.

The mountains of Lesotho are Southern Africa's most important watershed. A large project that involves selling water to South Africa is underway and promises to provide Lesotho with much needed income.

The two best ways of seeing what this country has to offer are by pony trekking or a 4-wheel drive safari into its most remote regions.

PONY TREKKING

Lesotho is one of the best countries in the world for pony trekking. The Basotho pony is the chief means of transportation in the mountainous two-thirds of this country and the best way to explore this land of few roads. Bridal paths crisscross the pristine landscape from one village or family settlement to the next.

The Basotho pony is the best pony in the world for mountain travel and was highly prized during wartime. It can climb and descend steep, rocky paths with ease which other breeds of horses would not attempt.

The Basotho Pony Breeding and Marketing Program is located at Molimo Nthuse about 34 miles from Maseru and offers escorted day trips to the refreshing rock pools of Qiloane Falls and other rides of up to 12 days in length (bring your own food). The ponies are well trained and a pleasure to ride. Accommodation on overnight treks is in Basotho huts or camping. The Molimo Nthuse Lodge offers accommodation (Class C) in a beautiful setting nearby.

The Lesotho Tourist Board offers a variety of all-inclusive pony treks throughout the country September-April. One of the most interesting treks is a four-day ride from Qaba in southwestern Lesotho to Semonkong and Maletsunyane Falls — the highest single-drop waterfall in southern Africa.

The pony trek begins after examining some interesting Bushman rock paintings and rock pools near Qaba. Riding east, the dark-blue skies are broken by high mountains in the distance. Basotho, wrapped in their traditional blankets and traveling on foot and by pony, offer friendly greetings and warm smiles. Riding in a cool breeze on a moonlit night in these remote mountains calms the soul and brings peace and harmony to one's spirit.

The nights are spent in traditional huts usually owned by the headman of the village, providing a first-hand knowledge of how the people live. Hikes to view Ribaneng Falls and Ketane Falls (495 ft.) are made along the way.

The final destination is **Maletsunyane Falls,** a few miles and a short ride from Semonkong. These impressive falls drop over 620 feet in a majestic setting. Scheduled flights on Air Lesotho back to Maseru are available.

THE MOUNTAIN ROAD

This route cuts through the center of Lesotho from west to east through spectacular mountain scenery to "The Roof of Africa." From Maseru the road ascends over "God Help Me Pass" to Molimo Nthuse and the Basotho Pony Breeding Station (see above). Between December and March colorful scarlet and yellow red-hot pokers (flowers) may be seen in this area.

At Thaba Tseka the good road ends and 4-wheel drive is necessary to negotiate the tracks that pass small villages and isolated herd-boys. After Sehonghong the route descends into the Orange (Senqu) River Canyon dotted with unusual rock formations, then climbs over Matabeng Pass (9,670 ft.) which had snow, sleet and icicles during my visit in April, and onward to Sehlabathebe National Park.

SEHLABATHEBE NATIONAL PARK

Sehlabathebe has the highest sandstone formations (including arches) in southern Africa. This park is situated on a high plateau with small lakes offering tremendous views of the Drakensberg Mountains and Natal. Sehlabathebe means "Plateau of the Shield" and has an average altitude of over 8,000 feet.

This 26 square mile fenced park has oribi, eland, reedbuck, wildebeest, baboons, and abundant birdlife, including the rare lammergeyer.

The best time to visit the park for game viewing, hiking and for some of the best fresh-water fishing in southern Africa is November-March. Quickest access is by charter flight. Land access is by a 185 mile drive across Lesotho from Maseru or from South Africa via Qacha's Nek, Sani Pass, or a 5-6 hour hike of 15 miles from Bushman's Nek Lodge. The park has a self-service lodge (Class D). Bookings and additional information can be obtained from Lesotho National Parks, Ministry of Agriculture, P.O. Box 24, Maseru.

MASERU

This is the capital and largest city with approximately 60,000 inhabitants, located in the western lowlands.

Some interesting day excursions from Maseru include Thaba-Bosiu (The Mountain at Night), the table mountain fortress 19 miles from Maseru with access from only one route, and the Ha Khotso rock paintings, considered to be some of the finest in southern Africa, located 28 miles from Maseru off the mountain road.

The best hotel in the country is the Lesotho Sun (First Class), situated on a hill overlooking Maseru, with swimming pool, tennis courts, health club, casino, two bars and a lounge, two restaurants serving excellent cuisine and very good service. The Victoria Hotel provides tourist class accommodation.

MAURITIUS

Mauritius is a favorite destination for jet-setters, celebrities and royalty from around the world, many of whom rate this as one of the best get-aways on earth. The combination of the cosmopolitan atmosphere, virgin-white beaches, crystal-clear waters, exquisite Creole, Indian, Chinese and European cuisine, chic hotels and service to match is difficult to beat.

This mountainous island paradise lies in the middle of the Indian Ocean in the tropics about 1,200 miles east of the southern coast of Africa. Incorporating a visit to this remote island with a tour on the African mainland or round-the-world vacation should be seriously considered.

The most appropriate and frequently heard phrase on this island is "No Problem in Paradise." Unlike many "paradises" around the world, the people here have maintained their genuine friendliness in the face of tourism.

This 720 square mile island has a central plateau with the south being more mountainous than the north. Much of the lush vegetation has been converted into sugar cane and banana fields.

The population of about 1.2 million consists of Indians, Creoles, Chinese, Arab and Africans. Hindu, Muslim, Christian and Chinese festivals occur with uncanny frequency. English is the official language and French is widely spoken, while most of the people prefer to speak Creole.

The island is known for the awkward Dodo bird which could not fly and was hunted to extinction during Dutch rule in the 1800's, and is still home to a few unique bird species found no where else in the world.

Creole cooking, emphasizing the use of curries, fresh seafood and tropical fruits are often served. Mauritian beer and rum are popular.

Mauritius has a tropical oceanic climate. The best time to visit this island paradise for a beach holiday is from September to mid-December during spring which has sunny days and warm temperatures. April-June is also good. From mid-December to April is very hot and rainy with occasional cyclones. June-August (winter) nights are cool.

The average daily maximum temperature in January is 86° F and in July is 75° F. Surf temperatures inside the reefs near shore are around 74° F in winter and 81° F in summer.

SPORTS

Hotels are spread out, so visitors spend most of their time enjoying the many activities and sports their particular hotel has to offer. In many of the top hotels, most water and land sports, with the exception of SCUBA diving, horseback riding and big-game fishing, are free, including wind-surfing, water-skiing, sailing, snorkeling, volleyball, golf and tennis. Barbecues are also popular.

Big game fish, including blue marlin (plentiful), black marlin (world's record), tuna, jackfish, wahoo, barracuda, yellow fin and sea bass can be caught within a few miles off shore. An international fishing tournament is held every year in December; the best fishing is from December-March. Boats can be hired through your hotel or travel agencies and should be booked well in advance during this season. Fishing in the lagoons during this period is also very good.

There are colorful coral reefs and dozens of wrecks harboring a great variety of sealife on which to dive. The best conditions for SCUBA diving and sailing are October-March.

EXCURSIONS

The beaches, water sports, fabulous holiday hotels and exquisite dining are by far the major attractions of the island. In addition, there are many interesting excursions.

Port Louis is the chief harbor and capital city with a population of approximately 165,000. It has a large market selling indigenous fruits and vegetables, pareos (colorful cloth wraps) and other clothing and souvenirs. Chinatown is also worth a visit.

Curepipe is a large town located on the central plateau and is a good place to cool off from the warm coast and to shop. The extinct volcano Trou aux Cerfs may be visited nearby.

The world-renowned botanical gardens of **Pamplemousses** have dozens of bizarre plants and trees including the talipot palm which at 100 years of age blooms for the first time then dies, and giant water lilies imported from Brazil.

The land takes on the colors of the rainbow (on sunny days) at **Terres de Couleurs** (the colored earth), located in the southwest in the mountains near Chamarel. **Grand Bassin** is a lake in an extinct volcano, and is the holy lake of the Hindus who celebrate the Maha Shivaratree, an exotic festival held yearly in February or March.

Gorges de la Riviere Noire (Black River Gorges) are gorges in the highest mountain chain on the island offering splendid views of the countryside.

ACCOMMODATION

The St. Geran Sun (Deluxe) is a hotel resort of the highest standard with an international flair unmatched on the island. If you are going to see anyone famous while on this island it will probably be here. Other facilities include an elegant disco, casino, 9-hole golf course, sailing and SCUBA diving.

Le Touessrok Sun Hotel (Deluxe) is a splendid deluxe holiday hotel situated on the east coast south of the St. Geran. Facilities include two swimming pools, two superb restaurants, disco, shops, and beauty parlor. What truly sets this resort apart from the rest is the pristine Ile-aux-Cerfs. Guests have complimentary transfers by boat to this "Isle of Stags" with miles of the most beautiful beaches on the island.

La Piroque Sun (First Class) is located on a fine white beach on the island's west coast. Thatched cottages spread out from the main building which has a distinctive sail-like roof and the island's largest swimming pool.

The Merville Hotel (Tourist Class) is a comfortable hotel situated on a good beach on Grand Bay near the northern tip of the island. The Merville offers fine food, friendly atmosphere, swimming pool and all the usual water sports for its guests.

Le Chaland Hotel (Tourist Class) is conveniently located four miles from the international airport on Blue Bay on the southeastern coast. This bungalow hotel has a fine beach and all the usual water sports along with tennis and horseback riding.

SWAZILAND

Swaziland, along with Lesotho and Morocco, is one of the last three remaining kingdoms in Africa. The country is deeply rooted in tradition, an important part of present-day life.

Though Swaziland is the second smallest country in Africa, within its boundaries lie every type of African terrain except desert. Swaziland has five wildlife reserves, bushmen paintings, international-class resorts, and superb scenery.

The people are called Swazi(s), and the population of about 750,000 live in an area the size of New Jersey. The official languages are English and siSwati; English is widely spoken.

Only four rulers in modern times have reigned over 60 years: Queen Victoria of Great Britain, Louis the Fourteenth of France, Karl Friedrich the Grand Duke of Badan, and Sobhuza the Second of Swaziland, who died in 1982.

Most Swazi are subsistence farmers, following a mixture of Christian and indigenous beliefs. Most live in scattered homesteads instead of concentrating themselves in villages and cities.

Summer (October-March) is rainy and humid, with the hottest and wettest time of the year being December-February. Winter (April-September) is crisp and clear, with occasional frosts in the highvelt (higher altitudes).

Geographically, the country is divided into four belts of about the same width, running roughly north to south: the mountainous highvelt in the west, the hilly middlevelt, the Lubombo Plateau along the eastern border, and the lowvelt bush.

The combination of friendly people, interesting culture, beautiful countryside and small game reserves make Swaziland an attractive country to visit.

WILDLIFE AND WILDLIFE AREAS

Swazi reserves are among the smallest on the continent, but for their size contain a great variety of species. One or two half-day safaris by vehicle are sufficient for each reserve. The parks are ideal for horseback or walking safaris, providing close contact with nature. The country is host to more than 450 different bird species.

The Swaziland National Trust Commission (P.O. Box 75, Mbabane, tel: 42579) is in charge of the national parks and may be contacted for further information and assistance.

MALOLOTJA NATIONAL PARK

This is the country's largest park, covering 70 square miles of mountains and gorges harboring unique highvelt flora and fauna. Rock faces, rapids, waterfalls, grasslands, impenetrable riverine forests, and mountains provide scenic backdrops for game. Tree cyads over 20 feet may be found in the valleys.

Malolotja Falls with over a 150 foot drop are the highest in the country. Wildlife includes oribi, vaal rhebok, klipspringer, impala, red duiker, reedbuck, white rhino, black wildebeest, aardwolf, black-backed jackal, honey badger, serval, and zebra. There are bald ibis colonies in the park and Blue Cranes November-February.

With limited roads, the park is best suited for walkers and backpackers. Wilderness trails are well marked, and day trails may be used without permit. Camping along the trail is only allowed at official sites which have water but no facilities. Permits must be obtained for backpacking and for fishing at the Forbes Reef Dam and Upper Malolotja River from the tourist office. National park cabins (Class D) are available; bring your own food.

The best time to visit is April-June; July-August is cold but otherwise good; February-March is the worst time to visit.

The main gate is located about 22 miles northwest of Mbabane on the road to Piggs Peak.

MLILWANE WILDLIFE SANCTUARY

Located in the Ezulwini Valley, Mlilwane means "little fire" from the lightning which often strikes a nearby hill where large

Nyala

deposits of iron ore exist. This 17 square mile game sanctuary has a variety of wildlife including white rhino, giraffe, hippo, buffalo, zebra, crocodile, jackal, caracal cat, serval cat, civet, nyala, blue wildebeest, eland, sable antelope, kudu, waterbuck, reedbuck, bushbuck, oribi, springbok, duiker, and klipspringer.

The sanctuary is composed of Middlevelt and Highvelt with altitudes ranging from 2,200-4,750 feet. It is located on an escarpment that was a meeting point of westerly and easterly migrations of animals, resulting in the congregation of a large number of wildlife species.

The northern limits of Mlilwane are marked by the twin peaks of "Sheba's Breasts." "Execution Rock" is another peak where according to legend common criminals were pushed to their deaths.

Visitors are not allowed out of their vehicles unless accompanied by a guide. Guided tours in open vehicles, on foot, or on horseback can be arranged in advance at the Rest Camp. Horseback riding safaris are conducted along bridal trails through the park. The rainy season is October-April. Park bandas (Class D) are available.

EZULWINI VALLEY

The Ezulwini Valley, or "place of heaven," is the entertainment center of the country and is the most convenient area in which to stay when visiting the Mlilwane Wildlife Sanctuary.

At the heart of this playground is the Swazi Sun Hotel (Deluxe). Situated on 100 acres, the Royal Swazi provides accommodation with swimming pool, sauna, hot tub, casino, adult cinema, 72-par golf course, horseback riding, tennis, squash, mini-golf, lawn-bowling, casino, a discotheque, night-club, and cabaret.

Linked to the Royal Swazi by hotel bus service are the Ezulwini Sun Cabanas (First Class) with Swazi dancing every Saturday and the Lugogo Sun Cabanas (First Class). Guests of both hotels may use the facilities of the more exclusive Royal Swazi. Accommodation is also available at the Diamond Valley Motel and Mantenga Falls Hotel (Tourist Class).

OTHER ATTRACTIONS

Lobamba is the spiritual and legislative capital of the

country. The Queen Mother's village is situated here. A good museum concentrating on Swazi culture and traditions and the House of Parliament may be visited. The colorful Reed Dance is performed in the Somhlolo National Stadium.

Piggs Peak, located in one of the most scenic areas of the country, was named after William Pigg discovered gold there in January of 1884. Nearby is the country's most famous Bushmen painting, located at the **Nsangwini Shelter**. Ask the District Officer at Piggs Peak to find a guide to take you there.

Nhlangano means "The Meeting Place of the Kings" commemorating the meeting between King Sobhuza the Second and King George the Sixth in 1947. Nhlangano is located in the southwestern part of the country in an unspoiled mountainous area and once the burial place of many Swazi kings. The Nhlangano Sun (First Class) is the best hotel in the area, with casino, disco bar, swimming pool, squash and tennis.

SAFARI GLOSSARY

banda — a basic shelter or hut, often constructed of reeds, bamboo, grass, etc.

boma — a place of shelter, a fortified place, enclosure, community (East Africa).

camp — camping sites; also refers to lodging in chalets, bungalows or tents in a remote location.

calving season — period when births of a particular species occur. Not all species have calving seasons. Most calving seasons occur shortly after the rainy season commences. Calving seasons can also differ for the same species from one park or reserve to another.

caravan — a trailer.

carrion — remains of dead animals.

carnivore — an animal that lives by consuming the flesh of other animals.

diurnal — animals active during the day.

grazer — an animal that eats grass.

habitat — an animal or plant's surroundings that has everything it needs in order to live.

herbivore — an animal that consumes plant matter for food.

hide — a camouflaged structure from which one can view wildlife without being seen.

kopje — (pronounced kopee) piles of boulders sitting above the surrounding countryside, usually caused by wind erosion. (Southern Africa).

koppie — same as *kopje* (East African).

kraal — same as "boma" (Southern Africa).

pan — hard-surfaced flatlands that collect water in the rainy season.

mammals — warm-blooded animals that produce milk for their young, which are usually born alive.

nocturnal — animals active by night.

predator — an animal that hunts and kills other animals for food.

prey — animals hunted by predators for food.

pride — a group or family of lions.

rondavel — a round African-style structure for accommodation (Southern African).

scavenger — an animal living from carrion or remains of animals killed by predators or that have died from other causes.

species — a group of plants or animals with specific characteristics in common, including the ability to reproduce among themselves.

spoor — a track (i.e. foot print) or trail made by animals.

tarmac — asphalt-paved roads.

territory — the home range or domain which an animal may defend against intruders of the same or other species.

tribe — a group of people united by traditional ties.

velt — open land (Southern Africa).

FRENCH WORDS AND PHRASES

good morning	bonjour
good day	bonjour
good night	bonne nuit
How are you?	Comment allez-vous?
very well	très bien
goodbye	au revoir
mister	monsieur
madam	madame
yes/no	oui/non
please	s'il vous plait
thank you	merci
very much	beaucoup
today	aujourd'hui
tomorrow	demain
yesterday	hier
toilet	toilette
left	gauche
right	droite
I want	Je désire . . .
How much?	Combien?
How many?	Combien?
Where is?	Ou est . . .?
When?	Quand?
to eat	manger
food	nourriture
water	eau
coffee	café
tea	the
milk	lait
beer	bière
bread	pain
butter	beurre
sugar	sucre
salt	sel
hot, fire	chaud/feu
cold	froid

ice	glace
antelope	l'antilope
baboon	le babouin
bird	l'oiseau
buffalo	le buffle
cheetah	le guépard
crocodile	le crocodile
elephant	l'éléphant
gazelle	la gazelle
giraffe	la girafe
gorilla	le gorille
hippo	l'hippopotame
hyena	l'hyéne
jackal	le chacal
leopard	le leopard
lion	le lion
monkey	le singe
ostrich	l'autruche
rhino	le rhinocéros
snake	la palette
wildebeest	le gnou
zebra	le zebre
one	un
two	deux
three	trois
four	quatre
five	cinq
six	six
seven	sept
eight	huit
nine	neuf
ten	dix
eleven	onze
twenty	vingt
thirty	trente
forty	quarante
fifty	cinquante
sixty	soixante

seventy	soixante-dix
eighty	quatre-vingts
ninety	quatre-vingts-dix
hundred	cent
thousand	mille

SWAHILI WORDS AND PHRASES

hello	jambo
How are you?	Habari?
fine, good	nzuri
goodbye	kwaheri
mister	bwana
madam	bibi
yes/no	ndio/hapana
please	tafadhali
thank you	asante
very much	sana
today/tomorrow	leo/kesho
yesterday	jana
toilet	choo
left	kushoto
right	kulia
I want	nakata
I would like	napenda
How much?	Pesa ngapi?
How many	ngapi
Where is?	. . . iko wapi?
When?	Lini?
to eat	kula
food	chakula

water	maji
coffee	kahawa
tea	chai
milk	maziwa
beer	pombe
bread	mkate
butter	siagi
sugar	sukari
salt	chumvi
hot, fire	moto
cold	baridi
ice	baraf
antelope	swara
baboon	nyani
bird	ndege
buffalo	nyati
cheetah	duma
crocodile	mamba
elephant	tembo
gazelle	swara
giraffe	twiga
hippo	kiboko
hyena	fisi
jackal	mbweha
leopard	chui
lion	simba
monkey	tubili
ostrich	mbuni
rhino	kifaru
snake	nyoka
wildebeest	nyumbu
zebra	punda milia
one	moja
two	mbili
three	tatu
four	nne
five	tano

six	sita
seven	saba
eight	nane
nine	tisa
ten	kumi
eleven	kumi na moja
twenty	ishirini
thirty	thelathini
forty	arobaini
fifty	hamsini
sixty	sitini
seventy	sabini
eighty	themanini
ninety	tisini
hundred	mia
thousand	elfu

THE SAFARI PAGES

THE SAFARI PAGES

CONTENTS

AIRPORT DEPARTURE TAXES

Call an airline servicing your destination, the tourist office, embassy, or consulate of the country(ies) in question for current international and domestic airport taxes.

AUTO ASSOCIATIONS

Burundi: Automobile Club of Burundi   2749
B.P. 1069, Bujumbura, Burundi
Kenya: Automobile Association of Kenya   720 882
Nyaku House, Hurlingham, P.O. Box 40087, Nairobi, Kenya
Rwanda: Auto Club of Rwanda
P.O. Box 822, Kigali, Rwanda
South Africa: Automobile Association   28 1400
of South Africa
Corbett Place, 66 de Korte Street, P. O. Box 596, Braamfontein, Johannesburg 2001, South Africa
Tanzania: The Automobile Association   21965
of Tanzania
P.O. Box 3004, Maktaba Street, Dar es Salaam, Tanzania
Zimbabwe: Automobile Association   70 70 21
of Zimbabwe
57 Samora Machel Avenue, P. O. Box 585, Harare C1, Zimbabwe

AUTO/VEHICLE RENTAL COMPANIES

AVIS: Offices in Botswana, Kenya, Lesotho, Mauritius, South Africa, Zaire and Zimbabwe.
BUDGET: Offices in Mauritius, Namibia and South Africa.
HERTZ: Offices in Kenya, Mauritius, Namibia, South Africa, Swaziland, Tanzania, Uganda, Zaire, and Zimbabwe.
NATIONAL: Kenya, Mauritius, Rwanda, South Africa, Zaire, Zimbabwe.

Hire vehicles in Burundi through the Burundi Tourist Office (see "Tourist Offices" listed below).

BANKS

Barclays Banks are located in most of these countries.

CAMPING

Sitting by a campfire alone at night in the bush is an experience not to be missed. The night becomes very alive. Suddenly every noise means something. Was that the lion we spotted on this afternoon's game drive? Could it possibly walk right into camp and make a meal out of me? You then realize that your imagination is again running away from you, and that you are safe by the fire. The Milky Way is in clear view, it's getting cool out, it's time for bed.

Official campsites are often very reasonably priced, but vary greatly in their quality of facilities. Namibia, South Africa and Zimbabwe have excellent campsites and recreational parks very similar to those in North America.

When camping in the wild outside any official private or public campsite, always seek permission of the property owner in advance. In most cases they will be happy for you to stay. In many areas, it is best to hire a guard to help prevent theft.

Do not sleep out without some sort of shelter. Keep tent flaps closed at night. Animals will almost never attempt to enter a closed tent unless tempted by food smells from it. Store meat or other food in your vehicle — not in your tent. While in your tent, if you hear lions around you that you wish would leave, shout and they may go away.

Shake out your sleeping bag before entering it, and your clothing and shoes before putting them on after a night in the bush.

CHAUFFEURED SAFARIS

For those who wish to travel on there own, a chauffeur or driver/guide is highly recommended for several reasons. A good guide is also an excellent game spotter and knows when and where to look for the animals you wish to see most. He can communicate with other guides to find out where the wildlife has most recently been seen. This also leaves you free to concentrate on photography and game viewing instead of the road, and eliminates the anxiety of the chance of getting lost, or any other unusual events that may occur.

CLOTHING/WHAT TO WEAR — WHAT TO TAKE

Countries close to the equator (Burundi, Kenya, Rwanda, Tanzania, Uganda and Zaire) have small differences in seasonal temperatures, with June-August being the coolest time of the year; the main factor affecting temperature is altitude.

Countries in Southern Africa (Botswana, Lesotho, Namibia, South Africa, Swaziland, Zambia, Zimbabwe) have more pronounced seasons, often cold (sometimes freezing) in winter (June-August) and hot in summer (October-February).

Casual clothing is usually worn by day. Dresses for ladies and coats and ties for men are only required in deluxe hotels and restaurants, especially at the Mount Kenya Safari Club (Kenya), and in South Africa and Zimbabwe.

Bring at least one camera and lots of film, binoculars, sun block, electric converter and adapter, small extension cord, phrase book and dictionary, diary, alarm clock, insect repellent (ones containing 50% *DEET* are the best), brown, khaki or light green cotton clothing including at least one pair of long pants and long-sleeve shirt, wide-brimmed hat, rain gear, good walking shoes, flashlight and extra batteries, two pairs of sunglasses, two pairs of prescription glasses (for contact-lens wearers too) and copy of the prescription, prescription drugs with a letter from your doctor verifying your need, medical summary from your doctor if medical problems exist, bandaids, motion-sickness tablets, medicine for traveler's diarrhea, anti-malarial prophylaxis, decongestant tablets, laxative, headache tablets, throat lozenges, antacid, and antibiotic ointment.

CLUBS & ASSOCIATIONS

Tips: Utilizing memberships in certain international associations and clubs (i.e. Lions Club, Rotary) can provide you with up-to-date information, help save you money, and lead to personal contact in Africa with people that share similar interests. This is an excellent and seldom used method of gaining insight into a country.

Bring proof of certification for all sports or activities in which there is any chance you may want to participate. This will facilitate rental of equipment or guest memberships in various clubs and associations.

United Kingdom:

Globetrotters Club, BCM/Roving, London WC1N 3XX. The "Globe" magazine is excellent for ideas on out of the way places to visit. Most members are well-traveled and will assist fellow members with information and in some cases accommodation.

Kenya:

Cave Exploration Group of East Africa, P.O. Box 47583, Nairobi.

East African Wildlife Society, Hilton Hotel, P.O. Box 20110, Nairobi.

Flying Doctors Society of Africa, P.O. Box 30125, Nairobi; tel: 501301. Medical evacuation insurance.

Kenya Divers Association, P.O. Box 9575, Mombasa; tel: 471347.

Mountain Club of Kenya, Wilson Airport, P.O. Box 45741, Nairobi; tel: 501747. Weekly meetings Tuesdays at 7:30 pm at the clubhouse.

Wildlife Associations:

African Wildlife Foundation, 1717 Massachusetts Ave., N.W., Washington, D.C. 20036; tel: (202) 265-8393.

African Fund for Endangered Wildlife (AFEW) and the Giraffe Centre and Giraffe Manor (Rothschild's giraffes), 1512 Bolton St., Baltimore, MD 21217; tel: (301) 669-2276.

East Africa Wildlife Society, P.O. Box 82002, San Diego, CA 92138; tel: (619) 225-1233.

Foundation to Save African Endangered Wildlife (SAVE), P.O. Box 4386, New York, NY 10163; tel: (212) 949-9821.

Fauna and Flora Preservation Society, c/o Zoological Society of London, Regents Park, London NW1 4RY.

International Union for Conservation of Nature and Natural Resources, Ave. du Mont Blanc, CH-1196, Switzerland.

William Holden Wildlife Fund, P. O. Box 67981, Los Angeles, CA 90067; tel: (213) 274-3169.

World Wildlife Fund — U.S., Suite 800, 1601 Connecticut Ave., N.W., Washington, D.C. 20009; tel: (202) 387-0800.

COSTS

The cost per day is most dependent on how comfortable you wish to travel — the level of accommodation, type of transportation used, whether you're on your own or on a tour, and the destinations involved. Deluxe accommodations and transportation are normally more expensive in countries off the beaten track than in the more popular tourism spots.

For example, deluxe (Class A) safari camps in Botswana are often more expensive than those in Kenya, mainly because many are more remote and cater to smaller groups. Transportation is more costly in Zaire than in The Republic of South Africa because poor roads give more wear-and-tear on vehicles and petrol is more expensive.

Packaged tours usually provide accommodation and transportation at a lower cost than purchasing the same services individually yourself. Contact your travel agent or Global Travel Consultants (see page 236) for current brochures and prices. On the other hand, a self-drive camping safari or a self-drive lodge package including a rental vehicle and an accommodation package can be as affordable and more flexible than a tour, especially in South Africa.

As in Europe and other parts of the world, general interest tours cost less than tours with more unique itineraries. Getting off the beaten track may be a little less comfortable and dip a bit more into the wallet, but many travelers find it well worth while. Personally I really enjoy traveling in areas where the residents seldom see people from the western world.

CREDIT CARDS

Credit cards are accepted by most top hotels, restaurants, and shops. American Express is the most useful, followed by Visa and Diner's Club.

CURRENCIES

For current exchange rates, call an airline servicing the country of your choice (see "Getting There By Air").

The currencies used by the countries included in this guide are as follows: BOTSWANA (1 pula = 100 thebe), BURUNDI (1 Burundi franc = 100 centimes), KENYA (1 Kenya shilling =

100 cents), LESOTHO (1 malote = 100 licente), MAURITIUS (1 rupee = 100 cents), NAMIBIA and SOUTH AFRICA (1 rand = 100 cents), RWANDA (1 Rwanda franc = 100 centimes), SWAZILAND (1 lilangeni = 100 cents), TANZANIA (1 Tanzania shilling = 100 cents), UGANDA (1 Uganda shilling = 100 cents), ZAIRE (1 Zaire = 100 makutas), ZAMBIA (1 kwacha = 100 ngwee), ZIMBABWE (1 Zimbabwe dollar = 100 cents).

The malote (Lesotho) and the lilangeni (Swaziland) are on par with the South African rand.

CURRENCY RESTRICTIONS

Most countries require visitors to complete currency declaration forms upon arrival in which all foreign currency, travelers checks and other negotiable instruments must be recorded. These forms must be surrendered on departure.

The maximum amount of local currency that may be imported or exported is strictly enforced. Check for current restrictions.

CUSTOMS

U.S. Customs:

Travelers to the countries included in this guide may qualify for additional allowances through the Generalized System of Preferences (GSP). Contact your nearest customs office and ask for the leaflet "GSP & The Traveler," and for the usual duty free allowances currently allowed.

For current information on products made from endangered species of wildlife that are not allowed to be imported, contact the U.S. Fish and Wildlife Service, Dept. of the Interior, Washington, D.C. 20240, tel: (718) 917-1707, and ask for their leaflet "Pets, Wildlife, U.S. Customs," Regulation parts 17 and 23 for current restrictions.

Canadian Customs:

For information on current Canadian customs requirements, ask for the brochure "I Declare" from your local customs office. For restrictions on products made from endangered wildlife, request "Don't Bring it Back" from Agriculture Canada, Ottawa, Ontario K1A OC7. Further information on endangered species is available from Environment Canada, Ottawa, Ontario, K1A OC3.

African Customs:

Contact the nearest tourist office or embassy for current duty-free allowances in the country which you intend visiting.

DIPLOMATIC REPRESENTATIVES OF AFRICAN COUNTRIES

Embassies in the United States:

Botswana (202) 244-4990
Suite 404, 4301 Connecticut Ave., N.W., Washington, D.C. 20008
Burundi (202) 343-2574
Suite 212, 2233 Wisconsin Ave., N.W. Washington, D.C. 20007
Kenya (202) 387-6101
2249 R. St., N.W., Washington, D.C. 20008. Consulates in Beverly Hills and New York.
Lesotho (202) 462-4190
1601 Connecticut Ave., N.W., Washington, D.C. 20008
Mauritius (202) 244-1491
4310 Connecticut Ave., N.W., Washington, D.C. 20008
Rwanda (202) 232-2882
1714 New Hampshire Ave., N.W., Washington D.C. 20008
South Africa (also for Namibia) (202) 232-4400
3051 Massachusetts Ave., N.W., Washington, D.C. 20008. Consulates in Chicago, Houston, New York and Los Angeles.
Swaziland (202) 362-6683
4301 Connecticut Ave., N.W., Washington, D.C. 20008
Tanzania (202) 232-0501
2139 R St., N.W., Washington, D.C. 20008
Uganda (202) 726-7100
5909 16th St., N.W., Washington, D.C. 20011
Zaire (202) 234-7690
1800 New Hampshire Ave., N.W., Washington, D.C. 20009
Zambia (202) 265-9717
2419 Massachusetts Ave., N,W., Washington, D.C. 20008
Zimbabwe (202) 332-7100
2852 McGill Terrace, N.W., Washington, D.C. 20008

High Commissions In Canada:

Burundi   (613) 236-8483
151 Slater St., No. 800, Ottawa, Ontario, K1P 5H3
Kenya   (613) 563-1773
Gillin Building, Suite 600, 141 Laurier Ave., West Ottawa,
Ontario K1P 5J3
Lesotho   (613) 236-9449
350 Sparks St., Suite 910, Ottawa, Ontario, K1R 7S8
Rwanda   (613) 238-1603
Suite 903, 350 Part St., Ottawa, Ontario, K1R 7S9
South Africa (and Namibia)   (613) 744-0330
15 Sussex Drive, Ottawa, Ontario, K1M 1M8. Consulate in
Toronto.
Tanzania   (613) 232-1509
50 Range Rd., Ottawa, Ontario, K1N 8J4
Uganda   (613) 233-7797
170 Laurier Ave., West, Suite 601, Ottawa, Ontario, K1P 525
Zaire   (613) 236-7103
18 Range Rd., Ottawa, Ontario, K1N 8G3
Zambia   (613) 563-0712
130 Albert St., Suite 1610, Ottawa, Ontario K1P 5G4
Zimbabwe   (613) 237-0388
112 Kent St., Suite 915, Place de Ville, Tower B, Ottawa,
Ontario, K1P 5P2

DIPLOMATIC REPRESENTATIVES IN AFRICA

United States Embassies:

Botswana: P.O. Box 90, Gaborone; tel: 353982.
Burundi: B.P. 1720, Bujumbura; tel: 3454.
Kenya: Embassy Building, Haile Selassie & Moi Avenues, P. O.
Box 30137, Nairobi, tel: 334141/720961.
Lesotho: P.O. Box MS 333, Maseru; tel: 22666.
Mauritius: Rogers House, John Kennedy St., Port Louis; tel:
23218.
Namibia: see South Africa
Rwanda: Blvd. de la Revolution, Kigali; tel: 5601.
South Africa: 225 Pretorius St., Pretoria; tel: 284266.
Swaziland: Warner St., Mbabane; tel: 22281.

Tanzania: 36 Laibon Road, P.O. Box 9123, Dar es Salaam, tel: 68894. Consulate: P.O. Box 4, Zanzibar.
Uganda: British High Commission Blgd., 10/12 Parliament Ave., tel: 259791.
Zaire: 310 Av. des Aviateurs, Kinshasa; tel: 25881.
Zambia: Independence & United National Aves., P.O. Box 31617, Lusaka; tel: 214911.
Zimbabwe: 78 Enterprise Rd., Highlands, Harare;
tel: 791586/7/8.

Canadian High Commissions:

Kenya: Comcraft House, Haile Selassie Ave., P.O. Box 30481, Nairobi; tel: 334033.
Mauritius: c/o Blanche Birger Co., Ltd., Port Louis; tel: 20821.
Namibia: (see South Africa)
South Africa: Nedbank Plaza, 856 Kingsleys Center, Deatrix St., Arcadia, Pretoria 0007; tel: 287062.
Tanzania: Pan African Insurance Bldg., P.O. Box 1022, Dar es Salaam; tel: 20651.
Zaire: Edifice Shell, P.O. Box 8341, Kinshasa; tel: 22706.
Zambia: Barclays Bank, North End Branch, Cairo Road, P.O. Box 31313, Lusaka; tel: 216161.
Zimbabwe: 45 Bainef Ave., P.O. Box 1430, Harare; tel: 793801.

DRIVING IN AFRICA

One of the most adventurous ways of seeing the continent is to rent or buy a vehicle and hit the road — or dirt track, depending on your destination. A self-drive safari can be a real adventure, but one must be aware of what they are getting into.

Will a 2-wheel drive vehicle suit your purposes? If not, are you familiar with 4-wheel drive vehicles? Game viewing from a chauffeured vehicle is exciting, but driving up to your own herd of elephant or pride of lion is something else! This certainly isn't for everyone, and is not recommended for the faint at heart or people with little or no experience in the great outdoors. However, using common sense, studying up a bit on animal habits, and talking to the rangers you should be all right.

The following story may give you an idea of the problems that could be encountered. One April we rented a Suzuki 4-wheel drive truck and drove around Kenya. We entered Tsavo West National Park near Taveta in the south and drove northwards toward Kilaguni Lodge. Heavy rains caused flash-floods, turning streams into torrential rivers. One "stream" we had to cross had water rushing over the bridge as well as under it.

I walked out across the bridge to check the depth of the water, which was rushing so fast that it almost swept me off my feet. Deciding it was too dangerous, I studied the map for a different route. We drove to another crossing, only to find that there wasn't any bridge at all.

By then darkness had fallen, and we had to drive very slowly as to avoid hitting any animals. We returned to the previous bridge, only to find that the water had risen even more!

A decision had to be made. Our greatest fear was that the rushing water would hit the broad side of the vehicle and we would be swept right off the bridge and downstream, which would destroy the vehicle and leave us as easy prey to any and all predators of the night.

Something told me that we could make it, so I put the truck into first gear and drove slowly down the bank into the raging stream. When the headlights went under water I almost had a heart attack — thinking for sure that all was lost. Somehow we kept going, and what seemed like hours later (actually seconds) we drove up the opposite bank, and celebrated our success.

My point is that game viewing on your own should not be taken lightly, and only people with extensive experience with 4-wheel drive vehicles should consider it.

Circumstances forced us to do several things which should not be done in the bush. Getting out of a vehicle unescorted by a game guard is dangerous, especially near streams, rivers and lakes where carnivores wait for prey and hippos and crocs may be present.

The number one rule is to never drive at night. Never! Broken down vehicles and wild animals are often seen only after it is too late. And remember — driving is on the left!

Self-drive safaris are relatively easy to do in countries with excellent roads as in South Africa. However, in the great majority of Africa the roads are poor.

Carnet de Passage is required by most countries for taking your own vehicle across borders and must be purchased before arrival.

Self-drive safaris widely differ in cost according to the type vehicle, accommodation used and country in which the safari takes place.

For example, in Kenya a Suzuki Sierra Jeep 4x4 can be rented for about $450 per week with unlimited mileage, including insurance. On the average, about 620 miles is driven per week. Gasoline prices are about US $2.60 per US gallon and the vehicle gets about 18 miles/gallon, so gasoline would cost about $90.

Two people on a self-drive lodge safari should budget at least $1250 per week ($180 per day), and two on a budget camping safari at least $750 per week ($107 per day), for both.

Toyota Land Cruisers rent for about $42 per day including insurance plus $0.66 per mile. Rental and mileage charges for a 620 mile week-long safari would be approximately $660, gasoline extra. Add $10 per day for a chauffeur.

In many cases 2-wheel drive vehicles are sufficient for game viewing, and the rates are lower than for 4-wheel (4x4) vehicles. However, mini-buses or 4-wheel vehicles are higher off the ground and especially ones with open roofs are much better for game viewing than a car.

Be sure that gasoline or diesel is available in route, and carry extra if necessary.

Using the above costs for Kenya as a guideline, rentals in South Africa and Namibia are less expensive while rentals in Burundi, Rwanda, Tanzania, and Zaire are more expensive. For current quotations contact the agencies listed above under "Auto/Vehicle Rentals" or your travel agent.

In some countries such as Uganda and Tanzania, vehicles tend to be available for rent only with a driver.

DRIVING LICENSES

Contact the nearest tourist office or embassy and ask if an international driving license is required. Even if it is not required I recommend that you bring one anyway. International driving licenses are available from AAA and other automobile associations.

ELECTRICITY

Electric current is 220 - 240 volt AC 50Hz.

FOOD

European cuisine is usually served in the top hotels and restaurants. Tanzania, Uganda and Zambia occasionally have shortages of various foods and beverages.

Try a few Swahili dishes (East Africa), fresh seafood and Indian cuisine, especially along the coast. For tips on the best eating establishments in Kenya from the counrty's leading expert, pick up a copy of Kathy Eldon's *Eating Out Guide to Kenya*. Kathy is also the author of *Specialties of the House* featuring Kenya's tastiest recipes, and has compiled the *Safari Diary Kenya*, a series of articles written by authorities on subjects of great interest to travelers.

GETTING TO AFRICA

By Air:

Most all travelers from North America pass through Europe. Many airlines have stop-over packages at attractive rates, allowing travelers to recover a bit from jet lag and do some sightseeing. Many of the airlines below also have valuable printed material on the destinations they service.

British Airways (via London) services more countries covered in this guide and with greater frequency than any other airline.

Botswana: British Caledonian.

Burundi: Air France, Sabena.

Kenya: Air Afrique, Air France, Alitalia, British Airways, El Al, Iberia, Kenya Airways, KLM, Lufthansa, Pan Am, Sabena and Swissair.

Lesotho: Connect through Johannesburg with Air Lesotho.

Mauritius: Air France, Air Mauritius, British Airways, Lufthansa and Singapore Airlines.

Namibia: Connect through Johannesburg with South African Airways.

Rwanda: Air France and Sabena.

South Africa: Alitalia, British Airways, El Al, Iberia, KLM, Lufthansa, Luxavia, Olympic, Sabena, South African Airways, Swissair, TAP and UTA.

Swaziland: Connect through Johannesburg with Royal Swazi.

Tanzania: Kilimanjaro Airport: KLM and Sabena. Dar es Salaam: Air France, British Airways, Lufthansa, Sabena and Swissair.

Uganda: Sabena.

Zaire: Iberia, Lufthansa, Sabena, Swissair, TAP and UTA. Fly to Kigali, Rwanda to visit most of Zaire's attractions included in this guide (see "Rwanda" above).

Zambia: Alitalia, British Caledonian, Lufthansa, UTA and Zambia Airways.

Zimbabwe: Air Zimbabwe, British Airways, Quantas and TAP.

By Road:

From Egypt to Sudan and Ethiopia to Kenya and southward; trans-Sahara through Algeria, Niger, Nigeria or Chad, Cameroun, Central African Republic to Zaire, Rwanda and eastern and southern Africa. Allow several months. Roads are very bad.

By Ship:

Round-the-world cruise ships occasionally stop at Kenyan and South African ports such as the QE II (Cunard), Sagafjord, RM St. Helena Line, and Lykes Line (freighter).

GETTING AROUND AFRICA

See each country's map for details on major roads, railroad lines and waterways.

By Air:

Capitals and major tourist centers are serviced by air.

Botswana: Air Botswana services Maun, Francistown, Selebi-Phikwe, and Gabarone.

Burundi: Air Burundi. Domestic charter service only.

Kenya: Kenya Airways services Kisumu, Malindi, Mombasa and Nairobi. Cooper Skybird Air Charters Ltd. services Mombasa, Malindi and Lamu. Sunbird/Air Kenya services Amboseli,

Masai Mara, Nyeri, Nanyuki, Samburu, Lake Turkana and Lamu.

Lesotho: Air Lesotho services major centers.

Mauritius: Air Mauritius services Rodrigues Island.

Namibia: Namib Air services major cities and Etosha National Park.

Rwanda: Air Rwanda services Gisenyi, Ruhengeri, and Kigali.

South Africa: South African Airways services the cities of Bloemfontein, Cape Town, Durban, East London, George, Johannesburg, Keetmanshoop, Kimberley, Port Elizabeth, Richard's Bay, Upington and Windhoek. The "Visit South Africa Pass" is a real bargain valid for all domestic cities SAA services as long as the visitor travels in a clockwise or counterclockwise direction within a three week period. Comair flies from Johannesburg to Skuzuza and Phalaborwa (Kruger Park).

Tanzania: Air Tanzania services Kilimanjaro, Dar es Salaam, Kigoma and Zanzibar.

Uganda: Uganda Airways flies to Arua, Kasese, Gulu and Mbarara.

Zaire: Air Zaire services Goma and Bukavu from Kinshasa. Virunga Air Charters services the region covered in this guide.

Zambia: Zambia Airways services Lusaka, Livingstone (Victoria Falls) and Mfuwe (South Luangwa National Park).

Zimbabwe: Air Zimbabwe services Bulawayo, Harare, Hwange, Kariba, Masvingo and Victoria Falls.

By Road:

Major roads are tarmac (paved) and are excellent in Namibia, South Africa and Zimbabwe. Most major roads are tarmac in fair condition in Botswana, Kenya, Rwanda, Swaziland, and Zambia, and poor in Tanzania and Uganda. Burundi, Lesotho, and Zaire have very few tarmac roads. Many dirt roads (except in Namibia) are difficult and many are impassable in the rainy season (especially Zaire), often requiring 4-wheel drive vehicles.

Taxis are available in the larger cities and international airports. **Service taxis** travel when all seats are taken and are a reasonable means of travel. Deluxe **Express Buses** are available between major cities in South Africa, Zambia and Zimbabwe; less comfortable express buses in Kenya. **Local**

buses are very crowded, uncomfortable, and are recommended only for the hardiest of travelers. Pick-up trucks (matatus in east Africa) often crammed with 20 passengers, luggage, produce, chickens, etc. are used throughout the continent. Be sure to agree on the price before setting off.

By Rail:

Trains in South Africa are excellent, and the train from Nairobi to Mombasa in Kenya is also very good. Otherwise, train travel is slow and not advised for deluxe travelers. Train travel is possible from Arusha (Tanzania) through Zambia, Zimbabwe, Botswana to Cape Town, South Africa.

Kenya: Highly recommended is the overnight train between Nairobi and Mombasa for a real taste of old-time colonial Kenya. Dinner and breakfast are served with silver settings on this journey which passes Mt. Kilimanjaro in the night. Daily departures from Nairobi and Mombasa.

South Africa: Billed as the most luxurious train in the world, the Blue Train is truly a 5-star hotel on wheels. Table settings of silver and crystal, five + course meals, shoes shined while you sleep. All accommodation is very comfortable, with singles, doubles, and a choice of suites. The service couldn't be better or the staff friendlier. The Blue Train runs between Cape Town and Pretoria making several stops along the way, including Johannesburg.

SAVE (South African Visitors Exclusive Pass) gives a 40% discount off all first and second-class fares, and students get a 50% discount.

By Boat:

Steamer service on Lake Tanganyika services Bujumbura (Burundi), Kigoma (Tanzania), Mpulungu (Zambia) and Kalemie (Zaire) about once a week; steamers on Lake Victoria services Kisumu (Kenya), Musoma and Mwanza (Tanzania), and Kampala-Port Bell (Uganda).

HEALTH

Malarial risk exists in all countries covered except Lesotho, so be sure to take your malaria pills as described before, during and after your trip. Contact your doctor, an immunologist, and the Disease Control Center in Atlanta for the best prophylaxis for your itinerary. Use an insect repellent; those which contain 50% DEET are the best. Wear long-sleeved shirts and slacks for further protection.

Bilharzia is a disease that infests most lakes and rivers on the continent. Do not walk bare-footed along the shore, wade or swim in a stream, river or lake unless you know for certain it is free of Bilharzia.

Tap water is safe in many of the larger cities but to be safe it should not be drunk. Wear a hat and bring sun block to protect you from the tropical sun. Drink plenty of fluids and limit alcohol consumption at high altitudes.

For further information obtain a copy of "Health Information for International Travel" from the U.S. Government Printing Office, Washington, D.C. 20402.

HEALTH SERVICES

The Flying Doctors Society of Africa   (01) 874 0098
London House (AMREF), 68 Upper Richmond Road, London SW15 2PR, Great Britain
International Association for Medical Assistance to Travellers
736 Center Street,Lewiston, NY 14092
International Association for Medical Assistance to Travellers
123 Edward Street, Suite 725, Toronto, Ont. Canana M5G 1E2,
Medic Alert Foundation   (209) 668-3333
Turlock, California 95380

HOURS OF OPERATION

Banks are usually open Monday-Friday mornings and early afternoons, and sometimes on Saturday mornings. **Shops** are usually open Monday-Friday from 8:00/9:00 am — 5:00/6:00 pm and 9:00 am — 1:00 pm on Saturdays. Shops in the coastal cities of Kenya and Tanzania often close mid-day for siesta.

INSURANCE

Be sure your medical insurance covers you for the countries you plan to visit. Acquire additional insurance for emergency evacuation should your present policies not include it.

Travel insurance packages often include a combination of medical, baggage, and flight cancellation — all of which are highly recommended. The peace of mind afforded by such insurance far outweighs the cost.

LANGUAGES

English is widely spoken in all these countries except Burundi, Rwanda and Zaire, where French is the international language. Swahili is widely spoken in Kenya, Tanzania and Uganda.

MAPS

Michelin Map #155 (1:4,000,000) covers all the countries included in this guide. Excellent.

METRIC SYSTEM OF WEIGHTS & MEASURES

The metric system is used in these African countries. The US equivalents are:

1 inch = 2.54 centimeters (cm)	1 cm = 0.39 inch
1 foot = 0.305 meters (m)	1 m = 3.28 feet
1 mile = 1.6 kilometers (km)	1 km = 0.62 miles
1 sq. mile = 2.59 sq. km.	1 sq. km = 0.3861 sq. mile
1 quart liquid = 0.946 liter (l)	1 l = 1.057 quarts
1 ounce = 28 grams (g)	1 g = 0.035 ounce
1 pound = 0.454 kilograms (kg)	1 kg = 2.2 pounds

TEMPERATURE

−20° C = −4° F	5° C = 41° F	30° C = 86° F
−15° C = 5° F	10° C = 50° F	35° C = 95° F
−10° C = 14° F	15° C = 59° F	40° C = 104° F
−5° C = 23° F	20° C = 68° F	
0° C = 32° F	25° C = 77° F	

OVERLANDING

Overlanding generally refers to traveling mainly by land for several weeks, months, or even years, often covering great distances. You can overland on your own or join one of many organized safaris with groups often ranging in size from 8-30. This rough and ready type of adventure is recommended only for the most rugged travelers.

PHOTOGRAPHY

Consider bringing a small bean-bag to help steady your camera when shooting from the roof of your vehicle and a monopod (one-legged support). Vehicle vibrations can cause blurry photos, so ask your driver to turn off the engine for those special shots. Protect lenses with UV filters. Polarizers help cut glare and are especially effective when sky and water are in the photo. Store cameras and lenses in plastic bags to protect them from dust and humidity, and clean them regularly with lens paper or lens brushes.

For wildlife photography, 200mm zoom lenses are good and versatile; 300mm and 500mm provide better close-ups; 500mm are best in a dust-free environment because of compression. A wide-angle lens (28-35mm) is great for scenic shots.

ASA 64 and ASA 100 are best during the day when there is plenty of light. ASA 200 — ASA 400 is often needed in early mornings and late afternoons, especially when using telephoto or zoom lenses. Use a flash or ASA 1000 at night. Bring extra batteries.

PRICES

Prices in Africa as well as in other parts of the world can change quickly according to variances in currency exchange rates and inflation.

African currencies have been historically weak against the U.S. dollar, making Africa an especially attractive destination when the value of dollar is down against the currencies of Europe, the Far East, and other destinations overseas.

SAFARI TIPS

It is often better to sit quietly at a few waterholes than to rush around in an attempt to visit as many locations as possible. Don't just look for large game — there is an abundance of reptiles, amphibians, smaller mammals, birds and insects that are often fascinating to observe. Do not disturb the animals. Remember, we are guests in their world, not they in ours.

When on safari, leave your valuables in a safety deposit box at your base hotel. The less you have with you, the less there is to worry about. Carry enough money for emergencies, souvenirs, and what your tour operator suggests you will need en route.

Wear colors that blend in with your surroundings (brown, tan, light green or khaki), and do not wear perfume or cologne while game viewing; wildlife can detect unnatural smells for miles and unnatural colors for hundreds of yards, making close approaches difficult.

The very few tourists who get hurt on safari are those who ignore the laws of nature and most probably the advice and warnings of their hosts. Common sense is the rule.

Stay in your vehicle when in the presence of dangerous animals. Do not wade or swim in rivers, lakes or streams unless you know for certain they are free of crocodiles, hippos, and bilharzia. Fast-moving areas of rivers are often safe, but are still are risky. Also, do not walk along the banks of rivers near dawn, dusk or at night. Those that do so may inadvertently cut off a hippo's path to its waterhole, and the hippo may charge. Hippos are responsible for more deaths in Africa than any other game animal, most often from this type of occurrence.

Wear closed-toed shoes or boots at night, and also during the day, if venturing out into the bush. Bring a flashlight, and always have it with you at night.

Do empty out your boots or shoes before putting them on. One travel guide I read said this was nonsense, but I have met a few people who have gotten scorpion bites from such negligence.

Don't venture out of camp without your guide, especially at night, dawn or dusk. If you do stray from camp alone or with a friend, carry a large stick or pole. Lion in some areas still fear being speared by the local tribesmen.

Remember that wildlife is not confined to the parks and reserves in many countries. On my first extensive expedition to Africa I crossed the Sahara Desert and through Central Africa to Rwanda. After clearing customs at the Tanzanian border I began to walk to the nearest village that was about 15 miles away. One of the customs agents stopped me, stating that two men had been devoured by lions a few days earlier on their way to that village and suggested that I might not wish to feed the wildlife in that manner. Discretion being the better part of valor, I took his advice and a few hours later rode with a family whose forefathers had immigrated to the region from the Middle Eastern country of Kuwait.

A few days later the vehicle on which I was riding ran out of diesel just as the sun was setting. The driver said that they might be there for days waiting for fuel and suggested that I walk with two Tanzanian passengers to the next village, about 10 miles away.

This typical African night was so dark that I could not see the road beneath my feet. The two Tanzanians worked at a prison nearby and were in a great hurry to get there. When I asked why a prison had been built in such a remote area, one man replied, "Lions are heavily concentrated in this region. If a prisoner escapes, he usually doesn't get very far." Such words of comfort I could have done without!

Resist the temptation to jog in national parks, reserves or other areas where wildlife exists. To lion and other carnivores, we are just "meat on the hoof" — like any other animal — only much slower and less capable of defending ourselves.

A jogger was recently found on the rooftop of a deserted building in Chobe National Park. He had come across a pack of African wild dogs which were feasting on an antelope killed only moments earlier and realized that they could have just as easily had him for breakfast instead. He was certainly glad to see the rescue team arrive.

Do as I suggest, not as I do, and, most importantly, enjoy the adventure!

SECURITY

For an update on security for the countries you wish to visit, contact the Department of State, Washington, D.C. (tel: 202-647-5225) for their advisories on international travel.

SEMINARS ON AFRICA

Global Travel Consultants   (305) 781-3933

P. O. Box 2567, Pompano Beach, FL 33072
Seminars by Mark Nolting, author of this guide.

SHOPPING

If you like bartering, bring old clothes to trade for souvenirs. This works particularly well at roadside stands and in small villages, although the villagers are becoming more discerning in their tastes.

Botswana: Baskets and carvings are sold in Maun, Kasane and the Mall in Gaborone. Also consider products made from karakul fleece, pottery, tapestries, and rugs.

Burundi: Crafts available in numerous shops.

Kenya: Makonde ebony and Akamba wood carvings, soapstone carvings, colorful kangas and kikois (cloth wraps). In Mombasa, Zanzibar chests, gold and silverwork, brasswork, Arab jewelry and antiques.

Lesotho: Basotho woven carpets are known worldwide, tapestry-weaving and conical straw hats.

Mauritius: Intricately-detailed handmade model sailing ships of camphor or teak from Camajora or Jose Ramar in Curepipe, pareos (colorful light cotton wraps), macrame wall hangings and Mauritian dolls.

Namibia: Semi-precious stones and jewelry (SWA Gemstones in Outjo, south of Etosha N.P. is excellent), karakul wool carpets, mats, and wall hangings, Ovambo baskets, carvings of verdite, onyx and soapstone.

Rwanda: Beautiful hand-made embroidery from the Catholic Mission in Rutongo, baskets, drums and carved masks.

South Africa: Precious (especially diamonds) and semi-precious stones and jewelry, gold, karakul wool products, wood carvings and beadwork. Bring your passport and return air ticket and you will not have to pay the 12% sales tax.

Swaziland: Beautiful hand-woven tapestries, baskets, earthenware, and stoneware, and mouthblown handcrafted glass animals and tableware.

Tanzania: Makonde carvings and Meerschaum pipes.

Uganda: Few shops for tourists.

Zaire: Wood carvings.

Zambia: Wood carvings, statuettes, semi-precious stones and copper souvenirs.

Zimbabwe: Carvings of wood, stone and Zimbabwe's unique verdite, intricate baskets, ceramic-ware and crocheted garments.

THEFT

The number one rule in preventing theft on vacation is to leave all unnecessary valuables at home. What you must bring, lock in safety deposit boxes when not in use. Theft in Africa is generally no worse than in Europe or the USA. One difference is that Africans are poorer and will steal things that most American or European thieves would consider worthless.

TIME ZONES

EST+7/GMT+2
Botswana
Burundi
Lesotho
Namibia
Rwanda
South Africa
Swaziland
Zaire (Eastern)
Zambia
Zimbabwe

EST+8/GMT+3
Kenya
Tanzania
Uganda

EST+9/GMT+4
Mauritius

TIPPING

A 10% tip is recommended for good service where a service charge is not included in the bill except in Zambia where tipping is against the law.

TOURIST INFORMATION

Offices in the United States:
Kenya Office of Tourism
424 Madison Ave., New York, NY 10017   (212) 486-1300/3
Doheny Plaza, Suite 111, 9100 Wilshire Blvd.
Beverly Hills, CA 90212   (213) 274-6635
Mauritius Tourist Information Office   (212) 239-8350
401 7th Ave., New York, NY 10001

Namibia: see South Africa below.
South Africa Office of Tourism
9465 Wilshire Blvd., Beverly Hills, CA 90212   (213) 275-4111
307 N. Michigan Ave., Chicago, IL 60601   (312) 726-0517
747 Third Ave., 20th Floor,
New York, NY 10017   (212) 838-8841
Tanzania Office of Tourism   (212) 986-7124
205 East 42nd St., New York, NY 10017
Zimbabwe Tourist Office   (800) 621-2381, (212) 307 6565
1270 Ave. of the Americas, Suite 1905, New York, NY 10020

Offices in Africa:

Botswana Division of Tourism   53024/3314
Private Bag 0047, Gaborone, Botswana
Burundi National Office for Tourism   22023, 22202
Liberty Ave., P.O. Box 902, Bujumbura, Burundi
Kenya: Ministry of Tourism and Wildlife
P. O. Box 30027, Nairobi, Kenya, Information office in front of
Hilton Hotel.
Lesotho National Tourist Board   32-3760
P.O. Box 1378, Maseru 100, Lesotho
Mauritius Government Tourist Office   011703
Registrar General Bldg., Jules Koenig St., Port Louis, Mauritius
Namibia: SWA Directorate of Trade and Tourism   26571
Private Bag 13297, Windhoek 9000, Namibia
Rwanda: Office Rwandais du Tourism et des   6512
Parcs Nationaux, B. P. 905, Kigali, Rwanda
South African Tourism Board   471131
Mellyn Park Office Block, Private Bag X164, Pretoria 0001
Swaziland Government Tourist Office   4-2531
Swazi Plaza, P.O. Box 451, Mbabane, Swaziland
Tanzania Tourist Corporation   27671
Maktaba St., P.O. Box 2485, Dar es Salaam, Tanzania
Zanzibar: Tanzania Friendship Tourist Bureau   32344
P. O. Box 216, Zanzibar, Tanzania
Uganda: Ministry of Tourism and Wildlife   32971/4
P. O. Box 4241, Kampala, Uganda
Zaire: Commissariat National du Tourisme   25828
Blvd. du Trent-Juin, B. P. 9502, Kinshasa, Zaire
Centre d'Accueil du Tourisme, Blvd. Mobutu, B.P. 242, Goma,
Zaire. Also contact Sabena Airlines for information.

Zambia National Tourist Board	
Cairo Rd., P. O. Box 30017, Lusaka, Zambia	217761
Mosi-oa-Tunya Rd., P.O. Box 60342,	
Livingstone, Zambia	3534/5
Zimbabwe Tourist Development Corporation	793666/7/8/9
P. O. Box 8052, Harare, Zimbabwe	

TRAVEL CONSULTANTS SPECIALIZING IN AFRICA

Global Travel Consultants, P. O. Box 2567, Pompano Beach, FL 33072; tel: (305) 781-3933. Featuring travel expert Mark Nolting.

TRAVELERS CHECKS

American Express Traveler's Checks are widely accepted, as are Thomas Cook's and a few others. Stay away from lesser-known companies; you may have difficulty cashing them.

VACCINATIONS

Check with the tourist offices or embassies of the countries you wish to visit for current requirements. Then check with your doctor and preferably an immunologist, or call your local health department or the Center for Disease Control, Atlanta, GA 30333, tel: (404) 329-3311, for information. Once immunized, you will be issued an International Certificate of Vaccination showing the vaccinations you have received.

VISA REQUIREMENTS

United States and Canadian passport holders must have visas for some of the countries included in this guide. Apply for visas with the closest diplomatic representative well in advance, and check for all current requirements (see Diplomatic Representatives).

WARNING: Visitors with South African visas stamped in their passports may be refused entry into some African countries. Call the embassies of the countries you wish to visit (do not give your name) for current information. The U.S. Passport office often will issue you a second passport in these circumstances.

Masai

INDEX

BIOGRAPHICAL DATA

Mark W. Nolting was born May 21, 1951 in Minneapolis, Minnesota, and moved to Pensacola, Florida, when he was four years old. He graduated as Valedictorian of Escambia High School and with honors from Florida State University with a bachelor's degree majoring in Business Administration and minoring in chemistry, mathematics and biology.

After working for one and a half years for a Ft. Lauderdale, Florida, marketing company he decided to throw security to the wind and pursue his life-long dream of traveling around the world. Armed with only a one-way ticket to Luxembourg and $840 to his name, he set off in October of 1975.

In December of that year he landed a job with ABC Sports covering the Winter Olympics in Innsbruck, Austria. With finances reconstituted he set off to explore the Middle East and Egypt, then returned to Europe and worked as a marketing consultant with a major German corporation in Hamburg, where he quickly became proficient in the language.

With the contract completed in December, 1976, he hitch-hiked across Europe to Africa, across the Sahara Desert and Central Africa to East Africa on less than $2 per day, often staying with the local people in their thatch or mud huts, experiencing their lifestyles first-hand.

From Africa he traveled to Iran where he was hired as a Drilling Engineer to work in Saudi Arabia. This proved to be a challenge since he had never seen an oil rig before in his life! He worked for a year, spending frequent vacation periods exploring Southeast Asia. In 1978 after traveling through the Far East, he returned to the United States $20,000 richer than when he left home three years earlier.

At that point he chose to relocate in Los Angeles to pursue a career in acting. Over a period of four years he appeared in numerous soap operas, prime-time television shows and movies of the week, but longed to get back on the road again to explore more of this fascinating world in which we live. He took a job in the travel industry and in 1984 returned to Africa to write *African Safari: The Complete Travel Guide to 10 Top Game Viewing Countries*. Africa had by far impressed him the most in in travels.

During this two-year journey he went on safari in dozens of national parks and reserves, climbed several mountains, went SCUBA diving in the Red Sea, worked for Chevron Oil in The Sudan, performed the lead role in a play in Nairobi, and was a special reporter for Kenya's leading newspaper, walked thousands of miles through villages and virgin bush, stayed in many of the continent's finest hotels, lodges and tented camps, and dined in many of the best restaurants.

He returned to Florida to complete this guide and to establish a travel consulting business. As a consultant, he specializes in counseling and booking travel arrangements for individuals and groups to Africa and any of the more than 60 countries in which he has traveled. He is a member of African Travel Association and the Association for the Promotion of Tourism to Africa.

ORDER FORM

PLEASE RUSH TO ME:

_____ copies of *AFRICAN SAFARI* at $15.95 each

Subtotal _____

Florida residents add 5% sales tax   _____
Shipping and handling ($2.00 each via U.P.S.;
$3.50 per book first class)   _____

TOTAL _____

Make checks and money orders payable to Global Travel Publishers (U.S. dollars only). Mail to: Global Travel Publishers, P.O. Box 2567, Pompano Beach, FL 33072, or call (305) 781-3933 and charge the order on your Visa or MasterCard.

Method of Payment: _____ Check/M.O. Enclosed

_____ Charge to My Credit Card _____ Visa _____ MasterCard

Card # _____ Exp. _____

Name _____ Tel: # (____) _____

Street Address _____

City _____ State _____ Zip _____

Signature _____

_____ We would like your African travel expert, Mark Nolting, to personally plan and book our vacation, expedition, business, group or incentive trip. We have enclosed a brief description of what we have in mind, or will call (305) 781-3933 soon to discuss it.

_____ We would like Mr. Nolting to speak to our club, organization, business, etc. We have enclosed details of our request.

Please tell us about your trip to Africa below.

(You may use this page as an envelope. See over.)

Cut along this line.

Cut along this line.

Fold here. Fasten lip on front with clear tape.

Fold along dotted lines to make an envelope.

Place Postage Stamp Here

re: African Safari

Mark Nolting
Global Travel Publishers
P. O. Box 2567
Pompano Beach, FL 33072

What Others Say About *AFRICAN SAFARI*

It's Rwanda for gorilla, Zimbabwe for elephants, and Uganda for tree-climbing lions in this unusual guide. But author Mark Nolting does not recommend this last country for everyone: "Although I have traveled through many parts of Uganda and have only been met with kindness, as of this writing, travel there is still very risky." Other helpful recommendations include bringing along old clothes to barter with and resisting jogging in game parks, where a person on the run looks to a wild animal like "meat on the hoof."

> *Book World*
> *The Washington Post*

First-time visitors to African game parks will find this book helpful because it summarizes the wild-life viewing possibilities of each country and park. There are general remarks on each country, followed by more specific data on each park there, including facilities, regulations, transportation, costs, and best time of the year to visit. Tables and lists classify animals by habitat. A section titled "The Safari Pages" gathers data on camping, photography, banks, clothing, auto clubs, tourist offices, etc. There is a "safari glossary," and French and Swahili phrase listings. Recommended . . .

> *Library Journal*

"African Safari" is truly full of vital information and is written in such a way that it is not just fact but personal experiences, animal sightings and special finds in remote areas worth your visit. The information on towns, cities, the people and culture are equally of importance. I highly recommend "African Safari" for preparation for a trip to Africa.

> *Keith Tucker*
> *Chief American Representative*
> *East African Wild Life Society*

A nuts-and-bolts travel guide indispensable to anyone interested in viewing Africa's magnificent wildlife

Jonathan Fisher,
Managing Editor
International Wildlife Magazine

"African Safari" is the first publication of its kind that is unbiased, up-to-date, and informative. Before anyone travels to Africa they should read "African Safari."

Alana Fried,
President
Born Free Safaris

Mark Nolting's book compares wildlife reserves in 10 countries, highlighting the best places to watch and photograph wild animals. Full of helpful hints!

TravelAge East

We have just returned from a photo safari to Kenya. We can't tell you how much our trip was enhanced after reading "African Safari." The book's description of the reserves and the wildlife of them prepared us for our trip of a lifetime. Thank you, Mark Nolting, so much, for the insight you gave us.

Betty & Merritt Epstein
Coconut Grove, FL

I took "African Safari" to Uganda, Zaire and Rwanda. Up-to-date information — not available elsewhere. Perfect for the medium budget travel, seeking adventure.

Tony Leisner
Vice President
Quality Books